An Imaginative
Approach
to Teaching

Kieran Egan

An Imaginative Approach to Teaching

JOSSEY-BASS
A Wiley Company
www.josseybass.com

Published by Jossey-Bass
A Wiley Imprint
989 Market Street, San Francisco, CA 94103-1741   www.josseybass.com

Jossey-Bass books and products are available through most bookstores. To contact Jossey-Bass directly, call our Customer Care Department within the U.S. at 800-956-7739, outside the U.S. at 317-572-3986, or fax 317-572-4002.

Jossey-Bass also publishes its books in a variety of electronic formats. Some content that appears in print may not be available in electronic books.

Library of Congress Cataloging-in-Publication Data

Egan, Kieran.
  An imaginative approach to teaching / Kieran Egan.—1st ed.
    p. cm.
  Includes bibliographical references and index.
  ISBN 0-7879-7157-X (alk. paper)
  1. Teaching. 2. Creative thinking—Study and teaching. 3. Imagination in children.
  I. Title.
  LB1025.3.E37 2005
  371.102—dc22
                                   2004020703

Printed in the United States of America
FIRST EDITION
HB Printing 10 9 8 7 6 5 4 3 2 1

Contents

Acknowledgments

I would like to thank the members of the Imaginative Education Research Group who kindly read and made helpful comments on this book as I was writing it. I had particularly useful comments from so many people that I fear forgetting someone: Anne Choda-kowski, Isabelle Eaton, Mark Fettes, Natalia Gajdamaschko, Stan Garrod, Joi Freed-Garrod, Monika Hilder, Geoff Madoc-Jones, Nicole Marcia, Teresa Martin, Marcia McKenzie, Amrit Mundy, Apko Nap, Dawn Popetia, Claudia Ruitenberg, Maureen Stout, and Keiichi Takaya. I am most grateful for the superb copyediting job by Hilary Powers.

Introduction

Imagination Underfoot

A couple of days ago, as I was sitting wondering how to begin this book, my two grandchildren were playing under my desk with some cardboard boxes they had brought up from the basement. I know that in fifty years I'll look back at such moments as wonderfully rich experiences, but at the time it was a bit irritating and a distraction, as I was anxiously trying to think about how to start writing about education and imagination.

Then Joshua said, "This'll be our house, OK, Jordan?"

"OK," said Jordan.

And then they began a complicated adventure that involved some "mom and dad" talk, and after about ten minutes had them emerging to ask me to cut out windows in one of the boxes, "and another bigger one for the door." The trouble with thinking about education and imagination, of course, is that you are inclined not to notice it underfoot! I realized that what had been distracting me was exactly what I was supposed to be thinking about. How do we bring that easy imaginative engagement of young children to the learning of algebra and history and so on throughout their years of schooling? That is what I think I know how to do, and that is what this book is about.

A New Approach to Teaching and Learning

The main idea here is that engaging students' imaginations is crucial to successful learning. If we want to be able to routinely engage students' imaginations in learning, we must understand the main tools they have available for the task. We must shape our lessons to take advantage of their current skills and help develop them further.

Imagination is too often seen as something peripheral to the core of education, something taken care of by allowing students time to "express themselves" in "the arts," while the proper work of educating goes on in the sciences and math and in developing conventionally efficient literacy. In the approach described here, imagination is at the center of education; it is seen as crucial to any subject, mathematics and science no less than history and literature. Imagination can be the main workhorse of effective learning if we yoke it to education's central tasks.

Of course, everyone knows that engaging students' imaginations in learning is one key to successful teaching. Over the years we have seen many suggestions for how to do this, but making its achievement a routine part of the classroom experience has proven quite elusive. The aim of this book, and of the Web site that supports it (www.ierg.net)—and of the series of books I hope will follow—is to make imaginative teaching and learning accessible to everyone in a new way.

This approach is unique in two important ways: It provides a new way of understanding how students' imaginations work in learning, and it does so in a way that suggests specific teaching techniques. This book includes frameworks and examples that support teachers in planning lessons and units that engage students' imaginations and emotions.

The mention of emotions might be a bit unexpected, but it is crucial because the imagination is tied in complex ways to our emotional lives. Students don't need a throbbing passion for learning algebra or a swooning joy in learning about punctuation, but successful education does require some emotional involvement of the student with the subject matter. All knowledge is human knowledge and all knowledge is a product of human hopes, fears, and passions. To bring knowledge to life in students' minds we must introduce it to students in the context of the human hopes, fears, and passions in which it finds its fullest meaning. The best tool for doing this is the imagination. This book is about how we can ensure this happens routinely in every classroom every day.

A Very Brief History of Learning

But getting to this new approach has not been easy. I suppose our educational problems began about a quarter of a million years ago—not that I intend to work up to the present year by year. According to the current evolutionary story, that was the period of the last rapid burst of brain growth in our hominid ancestors. This growth presented a particular problem to half the members of our ancestors' societies. The female pelvis had to widen to allow these bigger-brained babies to be born, but it couldn't widen so much that rapid walking would become difficult or impossible. For some reason, having bigger brains gave a significant advantage to these hominids, and so those with the bigger brains had more chances to have children, and so the brain growth continued. But there was obviously a limit to how far the architecture of the female pelvis could accommodate to what might well be an evolutionary advantage but was a major pain in childbirth. The pain has remained, but a solution of a kind was worked out.

The solution was that humans began to give birth while their babies' brains were immature, and the bulk of the brain's growth took place outside the womb. You can get a sense of the scale of this solution by comparing modern human brains and their growth with that of our chimpanzee cousins. Both of us have a brain of about 350 cubic centimeters at birth. As it grows to adulthood, the chimpanzee adds around another hundred cubic centimeters, whereas the human adds well over a thousand cubic centimeters, and most of that growth occurs in the first few years of life.

What is going on? What is the use of all this extra brain tissue that has cost so many of our species so much pain and trouble? It seems to be tied up with symbols, or at least a lot of it is. Unlike all other species, we are fantastically clever at associating sounds and images with meanings. Clever us. But this is also the source of nearly all our educational problems. Some of the symbols we learn and use seem fairly simple for us. Indeed, they are so simple that we *cannot not* learn them in normal circumstances. In a language-using environment, children cannot fail to learn the language or languages used around them. If two languages are in use, they will learn them both and hardly ever confuse them. Quite remarkable.

Language and Literacy

After a couple of hundred thousand years or more—I told you the history would move fast—people invented ways of representing language in written symbols. This is an enormously clever trick, later made even more useful by some people in the east of the Mediterranean who simplified the symbols to represent the sounds of language. The ancient Greeks brought this trick to even greater refinement by constructing a compact alphabet learnable by almost everyone. We haven't made any significant advance on their alphabet since. The trouble with this clever trick is that it both justified the profession of educator and left us with some subtle and not-so-subtle problems to deal with.

The not-so-subtle problems appear when we set about teaching children to read and write alphabetic symbols and recognize how they resemble oral language as a means of representing thoughts and feelings and conveying information. If we work hard at this, or make the children work hard, most of them can pick up the basic trick quite quickly. They can learn to read the oddly shaped lines and dots and squiggles as having specific meanings. But the more subtle problems become evident when we realize that this basic skill acquisition is only the beginning of the business of literacy. The more subtle problems are tied up with the kind and degree of meaning students can learn, and the problems extend even to such issues as teaching literacy so that students will enjoy engaging with it. If they don't find that the skill provides rewards of pleasure, of course, it will not develop in the ways necessary for what we consider some of the central purposes of education.

This might seem like an excessively refined thing for a teacher to worry about while struggling with the problems of ensuring basic literacy in unsupportive conditions. Working with students whose families read little, or for whom the purposes of education play little role in the life around them, doesn't often leave much time or mental space to dwell on how to make the experience return pleasure as well as utility to the student. The latter is often triumph enough.

Recent British experience gives a hint of why we shouldn't consider this too refined a problem. Enormous efforts were made, and largely imposed on teachers, to increase literacy scores. They were, over a decade, quite successful. Britain moved upward in those international comparative tests. But another survey result found that British children still score much lower than others in terms of the amount of voluntary reading they do. Thus many countries that now score worse than Britain in basic literacy have much higher proportions of children who actually read for pleasure.

And that's only one small slice of the problem, of course. The rest is connected to the enormous diversity of human knowledge and experience that is coded in symbols. The trick of literacy is one key to that great storehouse, but the storehouse has many inner doors and byways, and having the key to the front door allows one only into the front hall, not into any of the rich rooms that lead from it. Crude literacy tests often miss the subtle problem with which literacy has left us. They count as unqualified successes many cases where students can manage the coding and decoding skills that open the big front door of literacy's storehouse without being equipped to go into the further rooms where its great delights and power are accessible.

Theoretic Thinking

Well, that's the first quarter million years dealt with. We have learned two great tricks in the course of that time; one is communicating with oral language, and the other is communicating with symbols stored outside our bodies. More recently, we have learned a third great trick, which I'll call theoretic thinking. This trick involves abstracting ideas and theories from the particulars of any area of knowledge and manipulating the abstractions according to certain rules and then applying the results of that theoretic thinking back to the particulars we started from. You will be using this trick while reading some parts of this book. One problem with this trick, which we are only too familiar with, is that it is easy to zoom off into abstractions that don't adequately capture the particulars we want to think about, and then attempts to apply the results of the thinking are often worse than useless.

Doing this theoretic thinking well requires a person to begin by becoming very good at the first two tricks. The following chapters look at these great tricks in some detail—not analyzing them so much as illustrating what they bring with them and what they can tell us about how to educate our young, and not so young. These tricks are like master tools of our mental lives—like those screwdrivers that come with multiple bits designed to deal with many different kinds of screws. If language and literacy and theoretic thinking are three great multipurpose cognitive tools, it is also useful to look at a number of the smaller-scale tools that come with them. Or, in terms of the two metaphors I have been casually using so far, what are some of the multiple bits that can be fitted to these great tools, or what are the other keys that unlock the doors to the range of riches to which language and literacy and theoretic thinking provide initial access?

Frameworks for Teaching

Now these are very grand themes, yet this book is largely about principles of teaching and about practice, techniques, and frameworks for planning. But while it shows how the teacher can plan in such a way as to engage students' imaginations routinely, the techniques and frameworks are just means to an end; they are not the ends in themselves. The frameworks that I describe and exemplify are of use because they embody the principles of imaginative education. They are to be seen as crutches to help one take the first steps if needed. They are to help move along and show how the principles can be relatively easily put into practice. Once the teacher becomes familiar with the principles, then the frameworks can be left behind. That is, they are not to become some straitjacket for planning, but they are useful as reminders of the principles and the array of cognitive tools available for engaging students' imaginations in learning.

I should acknowledge that the drive for improved test scores is commonly seen as incompatible with developing students' imaginations. In times when educational success is measured in terms of high scores on particular kinds of tests, it may seem that developing students' imaginations is a luxury no teacher can afford. My aim here is to show how increased focus on students' imaginations will lead to improvements in all measures of educational achievement, including the most basic standardized tests.

A Map of the Book

The three main chapters describe some of the characteristics, or "cognitive tools," of students' imaginations. The first set, described in Chapter One, is made up of the tools that come along with an oral language. Chapter Two deals with a set of tools that come along with literacy, and Chapter Three focuses on those that come along with theoretic thinking. This breakdown is not derived from a traditional developmental theory, in which the characteristics unfold at particular ages. Rather it is tied to a new kind of theory of educational development (see Egan, 1997) in which the acquisition of cognitive tools drives students' educational progress. Most commonly the cognitive tools described in Chapter One will be found in young children before literacy begins to significantly influence their thinking. This tends to occur between ages seven and nine in Western societies, so Chapter One refers to children from the time they begin to use oral language fluently till about age seven, eight, or nine. The cognitive tools described in Chapter Two are most commonly found after literacy has become fluent, roughly between ages seven to nine and fourteen to sixteen in Western cultures. The third set of cognitive tools tends to be developed in Western cultures in the senior high school and college years, most fully by students who have picked up the previous sets of tools.

After each of the three chapters I have inserted a "half" chapter. These are designed to show the practical relevance of the cognitive tools explored in the corresponding main chapter. In the "half" chapters I show samples of moving from the cognitive tools to frameworks that can guide imaginative planning and teaching.

Two final points to conclude a too-long introduction: This book is describing an approach to teaching, so throughout I will be looking at the classroom from the teacher's perspective and emphasizing how teachers can use this material to make their work easier and more powerful. Similarly I will be focusing on what the teacher can do to encourage imaginative engagement and successful learning, and how lessons and units can be planned to achieve this end. This doesn't mean that I see students as simply passive recipients of teachers' work, nor that students can't become involved in the shaping of lessons nor in contributing in all kinds of ways. For economy of space, however, I will write almost entirely from the teacher's perspective, and leave it to you to see the ways in which what I am describing can be adapted to suit the active students we typically face in classrooms, especially if their imaginations are engaged in what they are learning.

And the final point is to assure you I will be describing what I mean by "cognitive tools" in more detail in the first chapter. And for that and other terms I use, the Glossary at the back of the book will provide a ready reference.

An Imaginative
Approach
to Teaching

Chapter One

A Tool Kit for Learning

Imagine you are in a completely dark cave and that you have a cane with which to feel your way forward. You push it at the ground and feel flinty stones in front, and to the side there seems to be something spongy, maybe moss, and further ahead something crumbly, perhaps mushrooms. What you actually feel is the impress of the head of the cane against the palm of your hand, but what you "feel" in some other sense is the flinty stones and spongy moss and crumbling mushrooms at the tip of the cane.

One of the things that seems tied to our remarkable brain development is a curious relationship with our tools. Many animals use tools of one kind or another: sticks to winkle grubs out of rotting wood, planks to reach food, stones to break shells. These are utilitarian tricks, of important but limited use. But humans' relationship with tools is qualitatively different; we seem to *embody* our tools in an odd way, or rather we extend our senses through them. And, even more odd in the natural world, as soon as we invent a tool for one purpose we begin to explore what other purposes it might enable us to pursue. We begin to heat up shiny bits of rock and a little while later we are sending robots to the moons of Saturn.

What is plain with regard to our physical tools seems even more profoundly true of our mental or cognitive tools. We begin to grunt warnings and satisfactions and a little while later we are singing Beethoven's "Ode to Joy." We begin to make marks on bone to record quantities of sheep and a little while later we are writing "Hamlet." The tools of language and literacy are not merely used for the relatively simple purposes for which they were invented, they generate purposes wildly beyond the imaginations of their inventors.

Let us, then, explore some of the developments of the tools of language. I won't be able to identify more than a few, but they are a few that I think are important for teaching and learning. These tools are not always used as well as they might be, and unfortunately are sometimes hardly drawn on at all—even though they are the tools that children can most readily use for learning in a way that can help them unlock the doors to cultural riches that lie beyond the great front door of simple literacy.

I'll begin with what psychologist David Ausubel calls an "advance organizer." He has shown evidence that learning ideas is improved if one begins by giving the learner some structured sense of what is to follow. I suppose "advance organizer" is a version of the old maxim that the best procedure for laying out an idea is to "tell people what you are going to tell them, tell it to them, then tell them what you have told them." I'll follow this good advice, and begin by listing a set of cognitive tools along with a brief description of each one. This list, or something like it, appears in each of the main chapters. These definitions also appear in the Glossary, along with definitions of the underlying concepts, such as *cognitive tools* itself, *orality*, and *imagination*.

Primary Cognitive Tools

Story   is one of the most powerful cognitive tools students have available for imaginatively engaging with knowledge. Stories shape our emotional understanding of their content. Stories can shape real-world content as well as fictional material. It is this real-world story-shaping that promises most value for teaching.

Metaphor   is the tool that enables us to see one thing in terms of another. This peculiar ability lies at the heart of human intellectual inventiveness, creativity, and imagination. It is important to help students keep this ability vividly alive by exercising it frequently; using it frequently in teaching will help students learn to read with energy and flexibility.

Binary opposites   are the most basic and powerful tools for organizing and categorizing knowledge. We see such opposites in conflict in nearly all stories, and they are crucial in providing an initial ordering to many complex forms of knowledge. The most powerfully engaging opposites—like good/bad, security/fear, competition/cooperation—are emotionally charged and, when attached to content, imaginatively engaging.

Rhyme, rhythm, and pattern   are potent tools for giving meaningful, memorable, and attractive shape to any content. Their roles in learning are numerous, and their power to engage the imagination in learning the rhythms and patterns of language—and the underlying emotions that they reflect—is enormous. They are important in learning all symbol systems, like mathematics and music, and all forms of knowledge and experience.

Jokes and humor

can expose some of the basic ways in which language works and, at the same time, allow students to play with elements of knowledge, so discovering some of learning's rewards. They can also assist in the struggle against sclerosis of the imagination as students go through their schooling—helping to fight against rigid conventional uses of rules and showing students rich dimensions of knowledge and encouraging flexibility of mind.

Mental imagery

is a tool of immense emotional importance, influencing us throughout our lives. In societies saturated by visual images, such as those of all Western and most Eastern countries today, it is perhaps increasingly important to allow students space to learn to generate their own mental images. We can easily forget the potency of our unique images generated from words. Often the image carries more imaginative and memorable force than the concept alone can hold. Together they can be even more potent. The use of mental images (as distinct from external pictures) should play a large role in teaching and learning.

Gossip

is often thought of as idle pleasure. But it can also play an important role in learning. Gossip represents one of the most basic forms of social interaction; it is easy to engage in and is usually pleasurable. These are not good reasons to avoid its use in teaching! It involve a series of skills, including the ability to fit events into a narrative, and can enlarge students' imaginative grasp of knowledge. Gossip can also contribute important elements to students' language, especially oral language, capacities.

Play   is a related cognitive tool, or set of tools. It helps people free themselves from objects with which behavior is often fused, as in, say, a classroom. By "playing school," for example, children can enlarge their understanding of the norms and limits of school behavior and get pleasure from parodying what previously had been a world in which they were constrained. Play can also enlarge students' self-control— and their understanding of the importance of self-control. In play they learn they cannot act by impulse but have to follow flexible rules, and they can pretend to cry while getting pleasure from the pretence.

Mystery   is an important tool in developing an engagement with knowledge that is beyond the students' everyday environment. It creates an attractive sense of how much that is fascinating remains to be discovered. All the subjects of the curriculum have mysteries attached to them, and part of our job in making curriculum content known to students is to give them an image of richer and deeper understanding that is there to draw their minds into the adventure of learning.

Embryonic tools of literacy will be picked up while students mainly use the tools of oral language, and increasingly the new tools will be engaged as students become more fluent readers and writers. We need to provide opportunities for students to begin using some of the later tool kit even if in embryonic form. In Vygotsky's terms (1978), this might be seen as drawing the students forward in their "zone of proximal development."

The topics listed here have been brought into focus by taking the engagement of students' imaginations as a central concern. If engaging students' imaginations is held steadily to the fore as a condition of successful teaching, then these categories represent the kinds of things to which teachers should attend.

This approach may seem a bit odd at first. It employs many unusual terms, and alas—possibly a major problem—it may seem as though it would make large time demands on teachers. I hope it will become clear as I progress that this approach isn't at all as odd as it may first appear, and it may even come to be seen as a more natural and sensible way to think about how to go about teaching and engaging students in learning. It should even save time as it becomes familiar. The following sections look at the terms in this "advance organizer" in a little more detail, relating them to the daily tasks of teaching. But first, it seems useful to discuss something of the nature of the category I will be using throughout the book.

Cognitive Tools

Let me slip back in time a little to introduce the idea of cognitive tools and how they work. It's seventy-five thousand years ago and a bunch of our ancestors are lying under a lean-to shelter built against a thorn tree, preparing to nap through the midday heat. In the deepest shade, lying on the softest fur hides, gently snores a man who is clearly held in high esteem by the small tribe. About ten years earlier he invented the past tense, which everyone in the tribe is now using, and that has been picked up by other tribes as well. In fact, it is spreading like wildfire. It is a neat and compact way to refer to events that happened long ago or yesterday. (Mind you, the rumor is that his daughters invented it and he took the credit. The daughters, now adult and more wary about intellectual property rights, have recently been working on the subjunctive and plan a public launch of the prototype in a few days.)

The past tense became a part of everyone's language over a period of time we can't even guess at. But it has been learned as a component of most languages ever since.

When the past tense is mentioned in grammar textbooks, it may look like a rule—but it's more productive to see it as one of our cultural tools. When we learn it, usually in early childhood, it becomes for each of us a cognitive tool, permitting efficient reference to past experience and events. It enlarges the scope for which we can use language; it enhances the power of our minds to communicate. Cultural tools, when learned, become cognitive tools.

Someone invented a counting system, creating another addition to our cultural tool kit. An individual who learns that counting system acquires a personal cognitive tool. Vygotsky described an array of such tools: language, numbering and counting systems, mnemonic techniques, algebraic symbols, works of art, writing, and the like. When we imagine these things as an accumulated storehouse of human accomplishments, inventions, or discoveries, we refer to it as our culture. Each of the elements of our culture can be internalized, in varying ways and to varying degrees, by individuals. From the storehouse of cultural tools we can select and construct our individual kits of cognitive tools. This imaginative approach to education aims to maximize for students the array of important cultural tools that they each convert into their own cognitive tools.

No one learns to speak alone—or to read and write or to think using theoretic abstractions. Each of us has a unique brain, but our minds are made up of all kinds of shared things that come to us only from living and learning within a community. As we learn from this community an oral language, then literacy, then theoretic thinking, we pick up three of the most potent tool kits available from our cultural storehouse. These tool kits are themselves made up of particular tools, and this book describes some of the main ones I consider of crucial educational importance and crucial to the stimulation and development of imagination. Although the storehouse contains another tool kit beyond theoretic thinking—which I have elsewhere called "ironic understanding"—its development normally begins only embryonically during formal schooling, so it is beyond the scope of this book.

No one learns to speak alone—or to read and write or to think using theoretic abstractions.

This imaginative approach to education emphasizes teaching and learning focused on the acquisition of the main cognitive tools that connect students' imaginations with the knowledge in the curriculum, on one hand, and enhances the powers of their brains in general, on the other. One important contribution that developing imagination makes to thought is to increase its flexibility, creativity, and energy. The aim of imaginative education is much more knowledgeable students who are able to think flexibly, creatively, and with energy about the knowledge they gain about the world and experience.

Story

All oral cultures use stories, and in all such cultures stories play a central role in the life of the society. Why should this be so? To answer that question, it's essential to understand what stories are and what they do for us.

So what are stories? I will tell a story in starkest outline and try to identify one of the most important distinguishing features of stories. To begin: "Jennifer walked into the rose garden." Well, what do you make of that? Not much, no doubt. It might be pleasant for Jennifer to walk into the rose garden; it might be her favorite moment of calm during her hectic days in the corporate jungle. But she might also be a notorious rose bush poisoner. Not knowing anything else than that she walked into the rose garden, one can't know whether to feel glad or sorry about it or what to expect next.

One needs to know what caused her action and what is caused by it. So let me add that Jennifer entered the rose garden to give her grandfather some news that would cheer him up. Now one might begin to feel a twinge of gladness: good for Jennifer, cheering up the sad old guy.

But as the story goes on, you will discover that this is a crucial event because Jennifer and her grandfather are major drug dealers, specializing in the youth market. The grandfather is sad because he lacks a specific piece of information that would enable him to pick up a ton of cocaine and deliver it to his network of distributors, who are poised to move it into schoolyards across the city. Jennifer walks into the rose garden to tell her grandfather the location of the cocaine.

Now, your feeling about Jennifer walking into the rose garden will likely be regret. If only she could have been prevented! But wait! I have to tell you further that the information Jennifer carries is a "plant" from her supposed friend, Marsha, who is actually an undercover cop. Jennifer's disclosure of the location of the cocaine and the grandfather's immediate attempt to grab it spring the trap that enables the police to arrest Jennifer, the evil grandfather, and their whole network of dealers and distributors. The key was to have Jennifer give the false information in the rose garden. Now, you will likely feel glad that Jennifer walked into the rose garden, springing the carefully laid trap.

One could perform the same simple analysis on a fairy tale, of course: "The hungry children came upon a lovely cottage made of gingerbread and candies." What a relief, as they were lost in the forest and starving! But wait. . . .

One knows how to feel about Jennifer's walking into the rose garden only when the story is finished. Indeed, that is how you know you have reached the end of a story—you know *how to feel* about the events that make it up. No one can program a computer to recognize a story as distinct from other narratives. The instrument for detecting stories is human emotion.

So the kind of meaning stories deal with has to do with emotions. Stories are instruments for orienting human emotions to their contents. That is, stories do not just convey information about events and characters, nor do stories just convey information in a way that engages our emotions; stories *orient,* or shape, our emotions to the events and characters in a particular way—they tell us how to feel about their contents. No other form of language can do this, and so no other form of language can achieve the range and kinds of effects that stories can. The story is like a musical score and human emotions are the instrument it is designed to play.

The great power of stories, then, is that they perform two tasks at the same time. They are, first, very effective at communicating information in a memorable form, and, second, they can orient the hearer's feelings about the information being communicated.

In an oral culture one knows mostly only what one remembers, and as the story is one of the most effective tools for encoding important social information in a memorable form, it is used universally. In addition, it can shape the emotions of the hearer to respond to its contents as can nothing else. Like all these cognitive tools, this one doesn't go away as its users grow older. So literate folk like us continually tend to shape our histories from a pure account of what happened toward some story that carries a moral about the virtues of our country or people, highlighting "our" beliefs and values over those of other countries and other peoples. We use stories constantly in our daily lives to give emotional meaning to what would otherwise remain, as it has been eloquently put, "just one damn thing after another." Stories shape events into emotionally meaningful patterns.

I can't know the conditions in which you are reading this book, but let's pretend you are sitting in a comfortable chair with a freshly poured cup of hot tea or coffee beside you, and a couple of chocolate chip cookies on a plate on a nearby small table. I know—dream on. At this point, let us imagine that you decide you could indeed replicate these conditions, so you go to make yourself some tea, let's say, get some cookies, sit down again to read on and see what else I have in store for you. You feel glad you are reading such a helpful book that is obviously improving your life, if only in this small tea-and-cookies way. Alas, in sitting back in the chair you topple the teacup onto your thigh, burning yourself rather badly. Sorry 'bout that. Now you curse the stupid book that has been a cause of your considerable pain. It looks so bad that you decide you had better see a doctor. She recommends a cream, which you pick up at a local pharmacy. On the way out, you decide on impulse to buy a lottery ticket. You win $12,000,000! Now how do you feel about the book that caused the spill that caused the visit to the pharmacy that won you all this tax-free money? (I'll settle for 10 percent.) You might even have the book framed as the source of your new wealth. (You certainly don't need to go on reading the thing now.) But the first thing you do is buy the yacht of your dreams, take it out for a first sail, and drown. Sorry again. Now how do you feel about the book that caused the spill that caused . . . and so on? That is, in life our feelings about events are always provisional, due to be changed as future events influence how we constantly reconstruct past events. Only the story provides us with the security of knowing how to feel, because stories end. It is this "sense of an ending" that shapes meaning (Kermode, 1966).

The value of the story to teaching is precisely its power to engage the students' emotions—and also, connectedly, their imaginations— in the material of the curriculum. There are two senses of the story. The commonest is that fictional form, made up of invented characters, which teller and hearer understand is not literally true. The second sense is perhaps easily understood in terms of the newspaper editor who asks a reporter, "What's the story on this?" The editor is obviously not asking the reporter to make up a fiction, but rather is asking the reporter to *shape the events to bring out their emotional force*. That is, the reporter is asked to select and organize the material in order to bring out the emotional and imaginative meaning of the topic. This is the sense that I will be mostly concerned with in this book, and the sense in which teachers can use stories routinely in teaching any content, without fictionalizing it in any way. The story is more a matter of the shape one gives to the content than of whether it is true or not.

Obviously, it makes sense to design teaching to respond to the cognitive tools that our students have available. So put this story-shaping tool into your kit bag for the time being, and later I'll talk about the many ways to use it in teaching and learning. Instead of thinking of lessons or units as sets of objectives to attain, it is possible to think of them as good stories to tell in order to engage students' imaginations and emotions. This will obviously lead teachers to think about the act of teaching rather differently.

In the imaginative classroom, teachers will always have in the back of their minds an impulse to look for ways to tell the story about the content of a lesson or unit. What's the story about this? If it is the problem of how to teach students to distinguish the spellings of such homophones as *there*, *their*, and *they're*, the teacher who knows how stories can readily engage students' imaginations will avoid the usual drill and repetition exercises, at least at first. Instead students might be told that there is a new family in the neighborhood and they have three children who are called, a bit surprisingly, There, Their, and They're. The trick is to remember the way they each spell their own name. The students can be divided into three groups, each given one of the names and the task of figuring out the character of the person from the spelling of the name. So Their, for example, is clearly an egocentric cuss, keeping his "I" tightly inside his name, and They're is . . . well, I'll later show how one could use the framework that incorporates these cognitive tools to teaching a lesson on homophones. But you may see immediately how the students when invited to invent characteristics based on the spelling, and then to invent a short story about them, will fix the distinctions in their minds.

Metaphor

Metaphor is the capacity, or cognitive tool, that enables people to see one thing in terms of another: "I felt like I was walking on air!"; "Feeling down in the dumps?"; "He pulled himself up by his bootstraps"; "The markets went south"; and the like. Most simply, metaphor involves representation of one thing as though it were something else. We constantly make this peculiar kind of substitution in order to give force and energy and richer meaning than can be managed by a simple literal phrase or sentence. We do not all use metaphor equally well, but we all have access to it, and the use of appropriate metaphors can stimulate the imagination and creativity in all subject areas.

I have, of course, been using a metaphoric sense of the word *tool* throughout, confident that you will attach precisely the salient characteristics of a mechanical tool to the notion of cognitive tool that I am borrowing from Vygotsky and others. It is slightly magical, after all. You clearly select the right attributes of a tool's utility, its powers to expand our potential to do work, its transforming of how we see ourselves when "en-tooled," and you apply these appropriate characteristics to cognition.

We can appreciate the power of metaphor, which is easily accessible to us as it suffuses our language at every turn. "Every turn," "accessible," "power," and "suffuses," for example, all involve casual uses of metaphor.

Metaphor is clearly one of the foundations of all human mental activity, a foundation upon which our systematic logics of rational inquiry also rest, or—a better metaphor—a ground out of which they grow. As Lévi-Strauss observes, "metaphor . . . is not a later embellishment of language but is one of its fundamental modes—a primary form of discursive thought" (1962, p. 102).

Perhaps surprisingly, it has been shown that the capacity to generate and recognize appropriate metaphors seems to peak in humans at about age four (Gardner & Winner, 1979; Winner, 1988). Thereafter this crucial skill seems to go into decline, with a slight spurt again during puberty, and then it's downhill all the way, not exactly following the progressive profile suggested by so-called developmental theories. It is prudent, then, to consider ways in which this metaphoric tool can play a role in the transition of children and adults to enriched understanding. If metaphor is important for imaginative activity, as seems undeniable, it should be an important educational priority to work out how to keep it energetic beyond the period of its usual decline and help its development. As a caveat here, I should mention that from a Vygotskian perspective this early fluency in metaphoric usage is superficial—unmediated. Vygotsky would argue that we need to work hard not simply to preserve children's fluency but also to develop the kinds and power of metaphoric usage as we grow older.

To get some idea of the influence and power of metaphor, you might try to construct a sentence that has no metaphors. Once you look carefully at the preceding sentence, for example, you see a graveyard of metaphors. I call it a *graveyard* (to use a metaphor about metaphors!) because what were once clever linguistic creations have become so much taken for granted, and read so literally, that it's almost impossible to notice their metaphoric essence. *Influence* comes from words that literally meant to "flow in." How creative an act it was to apply this sense of water flowing into some area or container to the way in which an idea might affect the way someone was planning an action. Or how strange, but apt and striking, it must have seemed when someone applied the sense of putting stones or wood together to build something—*constructing*—to putting words together to make a sentence.

We value highly those people who can generate new metaphors; they can offer striking insights and they simply expand our power to think. We value writers who can enliven our reading by clever metaphoric play. Shakespeare seemed able to generate vivid metaphors as easily as breathing, and this power makes his lines seem fresh and striking hundreds of years later. Einstein has described how his insights into relativity came through his seeing the cosmos as though from the perspective of a particle moving toward the speed of light (an example that might also be borne in mind in connection with the tool of mental imagery).

So the ability to generate and recognize metaphors is something that comes to all of us along with our oral language. In many of us, as our cognitive tools develop, that metaphoric capacity, that crucial cognitive tool of orality, can become desiccated and conventionalized. In our teaching, we will wisely seek ways to energize and exercise our metaphoric capacity. You can bet the farm on this one!

In the imaginative classroom, teachers will not only use metaphors constantly—which we can hardly avoid doing—but will call attention to them (as, for example, in the case of "influence"), discuss them, encourage students to recognize their own and reflect on how they work. Just once or twice daily—or even less frequently, as long as it becomes a consistent exercise—try bringing metaphors to conscious attention and analysis. The class could be encouraged to write particularly striking metaphors they have heard or used, and perhaps even vote on "the best metaphor of the week."

Binary Opposites

Here is another cognitive tool that people seem unable to avoid learning (if you can untangle the negatives). It is as though we first have to divide things into opposites in order to get an initial grasp on them; so we easily divide the world into good/bad, high/low, earth/sky, hot/cold, courage/cowardice, and so endlessly on. Holding onto such opposites instead of recognizing the complexity of the world can create problems. But we're unable to avoid using these forms, so we had better learn how best to use and control this further important cognitive tool that comes along with oral language. Those who study young children recognize how common such oppositions are in their thinking. For example, Bruno Bettelheim observes the "manner in which [children] can bring some order into [their] world by dividing everything into opposites" (1976, p. 74).

Binary opposites, as they are used in the thinking of oral cultures, are not necessarily precise opposites, but they serve to organize some topics and then allow people to make further discriminations. For example, setting up such oppositions as hot/cold or big/little provides an initial conceptual grasp over fields of temperature and size, and then one may make sense within these of a range of conceptual discriminations, like *warm, cool, tiny, enormous*, and so on.

Try to think about any major event in the news at the moment. Or imagine hearing for the first time about some dramatic political event on another continent. You will likely begin to orient yourself to the news by using such opposites as—most generally—good/bad; whether you feel it was bad or good that the event occurred. You will then no doubt learn more and mediate the initial binary categories, seeing some aspects as good, perhaps, and some bad. If you reflect on your thinking, I suspect you will find endless oppositions lurking around. While we need to be alert to their abuse—as, in our history, associating male/female with active/passive and dominant/submissive—we need also to recognize their great utility and power in thinking and learning. Additionally, of course, awareness and reflection on binary opposites can help to repair simplistic and sloppy thinking, and also recognize abusive simplifications such as the one just noted.

I recently read a newspaper account of a study conducted a few years ago that looked at the fate of winners of huge lottery prizes. Most people buy lottery tickets and dream of what they will do with the multimillions they might win. Nearly everyone assumes that winning will be the ticket out of the irritations and restrictions of their daily lives and into freedom, leisure, and sun and joy forever. The study suggested that almost the opposite occurred for most big winners. One of the points made was that most of us rely more than we realize on the routine structures of our everyday circumstances—those routines, the nature of our interactions with others, the calculations of what we can risk, and so on. One thing that happened when people won huge amounts of money was that all these secure routines were completely disrupted. After the initial euphoria, and the throwing in of the old job, and the buying of the big place in their favorite holiday resort, there was the disorientation of simply filling each day with no help from their old routines and environmental supports. Most of those interviewed in the study came to see their winning as a curse—a curse that no doubt those of us who haven't won huge amounts are willing to risk. Just consider for a moment how that newspaper account is structured on binary opposites. How many different opposites can you find in it?

Think of the classic fairy tales and consider what lies just below their surfaces. What is "Hansel and Gretel" about? It reads like a meditation on the opposites of security/fear. And "Cinderella"? Rich/poor or vanity/modesty, selfishness/altruism. "Jack and the Beanstalk" and the others? Courage/cowardice, danger/safety, wealth/poverty, enterprise/timidity, cleverness/stupidity, familiar/strange, and so on. It is as though young children begin to develop these powerful binary categories as soon as they learn language. And it isn't only children, of course. Apply this kind of analysis to your favorite TV show. Slugging it out just below the surface are these oldest and most fundamental abstract sense-making cognitive tools. What else underlies the classic Western or cops-and-robbers or sci-fi stories?

In the kind of fantasy stories young children enjoy so readily, the oppositions are relatively stark: security/danger, good/bad, courage/ cowardice, and so on. Two features of these opposites are clear; one is that they are emotionally powerful, and the second is that they are abstract. In a simple sense, language implies abstraction: "Language creates distance between the self and the object; language generalizes, transferring a unique perception into a common one; language transmutes realities into abstractions" (Coe, 1984, p. 253).

In a more complex sense, it has been argued that abstractions do not develop as a result of encountering concrete objects but rather that only by using abstractions do concrete particulars become recognizable: "concrete particulars are the product of abstractions which the mind must possess in order that it should be able to experience particular sensations, perceptions, or images" (Hayek, 1970, p. 311).

Well, this is a difficult issue, of course. But we would be wise to be suspicious of the simple claim that young children and people in oral cultures are "concrete thinkers"; the prevalence of this odd belief has obscured the sense in which they are also, and perhaps primarily, abstract thinkers. I know this runs against the grain of what has been one of the commonest assumptions of modern educational thinking and teacher education programs. But being the commonest assumption doesn't make it right. Indeed, the more one thinks about it, the wronger it seems.

Be suspicious of the simple claim that young children and people in oral cultures are "concrete thinkers."

It is useful to echo in passing Gardner's observation that "developmental researchers have been accruing impressive evidence that even toddlers can appreciate quite abstract qualities in the world (ranging from numerosity to animateness to various kinds of causality)" (1993, p. 182). Gardner cites Carey and Gelman's work (1990), his own study of "the unschooled mind" (1991), and Keil's (1989) study that shows very young children will sometimes override strong perceptual or concrete cues in favor of abstract properties.

We would be imprudent, then, to ignore this powerful tool that all children have to help them in learning. This doesn't mandate teaching them that everything is made up of binary opposites, but rather it might guide us to see how we can often introduce topics in binary terms so as to provide clear and comprehensible access to them. Once access has been gained, then we can mediate between the opposites and elaborate the content in all kinds of ways. But if we go for the elaboration before the basic binary structuring is in place, we run the danger of, first, ignoring one of the students' main tools for understanding, and, second, teaching in ways that give them no adequate hold on what we want them to learn. Sadly, this is far from uncommon.

In the imaginative classroom, then, we will expect binary opposites to be used commonly to introduce topics to students, and also we will expect them occasionally to be made explicit and to be discussed. This will be true for whatever subject area we are dealing with. If we want to structure a unit on "Properties of the Air" for Grade 3 science, for example, we might begin by introducing the fact that the air, which students can't see and which seems empty, is indeed full of things more varied and wonderful than all the objects students can see. If we want to teach about the transformations butterflies go through, we can bring forward the unusual combination of their early larval and cocoon lives being constrained in a small space, and that they eat continually, but when they become butterflies their range of movement is for many species incredible and they eat hardly at all. That is, by focusing on such oppositions in a topic we have one additional tool for making the subject imaginatively engaging to students.

Rhyme, Rhythm, and Pattern

All oral cultures had to press their store of knowledge into living minds. Consequently, the techniques that aided memorization were socially of great importance. If something—a healing herb, a technique for digging some rare root—was forgotten, it was gone forever. All oral cultures discovered that rhyme, rhythm, and pattern were effective tools in aiding memorization. If you ask English speakers today how many days there are in the month of March, they will most likely recite in their minds the old rhyme:

> 30 days hath September
> April, June, and November,
> All the rest have 31. . . .

They will recognize that March has 31 and not bother going on to the part of the rhyme that describes February's peculiarity. Such a rhyme is a rare holdover into literate times. If we forget the rhyme today, we can always consult a calendar. In oral cultures a great deal of lore would be preserved in forms of patterned sound, most commonly structured within a story to increase memorability further. The recitation of sacred myths, which contain much of the most important lore of any oral society, would commonly be done to the rhythmic tapping of a drum, or to a simple stringed instrument, or even to slapping a hand against a thigh.

Patterned sound helps to embed lore and ideas in the minds of hearers. This basic patterning is a small-scale form of a larger patterning, in which rhythms of despair and hope, of fear and release, of oppression, resentment, and revolt, of youth and age, and so on, are caught and reflected in language. That is to say, our emotional lives are also patterned, and we can use language to echo those emotional patterns in its rhythms. We might be wise to recognize that rhyme and rhythm pervade our language and lives. And what rhyme and rhythm are to the ear, so there are other forms of patterning that engage the eye and other senses.

In the imaginative classroom we will expect more attention to be paid to rhyme, rhythm, and pattern in all areas of the curriculum. Dealing with the topic of homophones, for example, one might add a rhyme to help students remember the different spellings of "there," "their," and "they're." The following verse comes with thanks to Mark Fettes. I use it not as an ideal example nor as a piece of great literature, as Mark would be the first to observe, but as the kind of thing that a teacher might have a few minutes of fun putting together. Memorability is important, and perhaps one might try to make such verses a bit shorter than this. But making up such verses should not be just the teacher's job; students can be set the challenge to show they have learned something by composing a neat verse that contains the information to be remembered.

> Three little words, called There, They're, Their,
> Went out to play and they came upon a bear.
> There didn't tremble or shake with fear:
> "I've a T in front, so I'm There not here."
> They're waved high its apostrophe:
> "Run, Mr. Bear! They're coming, you see."
> Their didn't weep or wail or cry:
> "And their guns are gleaming like my bright I."
> Bear ran off, to his own safe lair,
> And told his cubs of his terrible scare,
> While There, Their, and They're went home to tea,
> They're singing there still of their bravery!

And the teacher might begin to frame a verse for the "Properties of the Air" unit—the following took me eight minutes (and you'll probably wish I'd spent the time some other way):

> The air is empty, the air is clear;
> You can walk right through it without any fear.
> Except for those gazillions of muons from the sun,
> And endless decayed skin floating round for fun,
> And blobs of pollen bobbing up and around,
> And piles of radio waves that turn into sound.
> There's viruses and bacteria ready to get you,
> And tons of crunched up fly-poop—yuckie-yoo!
> The air is full, it's a massive stew.

If the teacher is able to put in the few minutes it takes to frame such a verse, the students can then be invited to improve it, or to do their own on the same topic. Apart from enhancing their language skills, such an activity will reinforce their understanding of the properties of the air.

It is useful for the teacher to remember that the human mind is fascinated with rhythms and patterns—in art, in the vibrations of strings that make musical instruments, in waves, water, and sand, in regularities in living organisms, in our own bodies and their fundamental rhythms and patterns, from heartbeats to waking and sleeping, and so on. Too easy to forget all this faced with the needs to structure a lesson on some topic, but easier to remember if we are putting the engagements of students' imaginations to the fore.

Jokes and Humor

The earliest joke I can remember was one of those question-and-answer exchanges that goes: "When is a door not a door?" "I don't know." "When it's ajar." Perhaps the reason I remember it after the centuries since I first heard it is the fact that I didn't know what "ajar" meant. I recall trying to imagine a door that looked like a jar, or a jar with a door in it, but nothing seemed to make sense, even though I remember my friend Henry Leach thinking it was very funny. Sometime over the following few weeks I discovered that there was a word *ajar*, meaning partly open. I was a bit slow on the uptake, but I bet Henry Leach doesn't remember it so well. Such jokes, incidentally, can help strengthen and enlarge our metaphoric capacity.

One consequence of literacy is that language becomes visible. Literacy moves language from a medium connected uniquely to the ear to one also connected to the eye. The particular kind of writing system we use profoundly affects the way we conceive of language (Olson, 1994). In general, we simply don't notice how profoundly this change affects our understanding of language. Literacy, then, enables us to reflect on, and become conscious of, language in a somewhat new way. Within orality, of course, there are also techniques that draw attention to language and help us to become conscious of it. One of these techniques is the joke. The joke about a door being ajar is indeed only meaningful in an oral environment. Written down, its visibility undermines it. For much of the time, it is useful to bear in mind, the classroom is an oral environment.

Often enough, though, such jokes can survive into a literate environment because they rely on homonyms. Their significant educational value, however, is that they draw attention to language as an object rather than leaving it as a more or less unconscious behavior. Once children begin to observe language as an object, they begin to develop that "metacognitive awareness" that seems to be important for their intellectual development:

Teacher: John, what's the outside of a tree called?
John: I don't know.
Teacher: Bark, John. Bark.
John: Bow, wow, wow.

Girl to magician: Can you pull a rabbit out of your hat?
Magician: I can normally, but I've just washed my hare and can't
    do a thing with it.

Traveler: There are some spectacles that one never forgets.
Cousin at home: I wish you'd get me a pair. I'm always forgetting
    mine.

Visitor: Where is the park?
Resident: There's no park around here.
Visitor: Then how come this sign says "Park Here"?

Jim: Should you eat fried chicken with your fingers?
Jane: No. You should eat your fingers separately.

Mary: Do you like raisin bread?
Peter: I don't know. I've never raised any.

Doctor: Did you take the patient's temperature?
Nurse: No. Is it missing?

Well, OK, sorry 'bout that. Perhaps not the greatest jokes in the world, but each has the educational value of drawing attention to language as an object that one can manipulate for purposes of fun—and, the student discovers, for endless other purposes too. But to accept the latent invitation that language offers to manipulate it, one needs to recognize the possibility. That recognition can be stimulated by particular kinds of jokes.

Jokes draw on various of the cognitive tools already mentioned. They often rely on metaphoric connections and are commonly a kind of mini story, or they suggest a story that is going on outside the joke. They can also enlarge our repertoire of expectations, and make more complex the range of emotional rhythms we can anticipate. The pompous person slipping on a banana skin is a compact form of endless more elaborate jokes that provide a quick laugh along with a more persistent moral lesson.

One of the damages of literacy is what we call—for good reasons—literal thinking. This is thinking that gets caught up with some logical principle and follows it at the expense of the greater fluidity and complexity of reality. One sees it too commonly in people who replace complex reality with their limited rigid idea and simply refuse to acknowledge what won't fit their scheme. Humor is the great solvent and disrupter of excessive literalness in thinking.

Children's everyday lives are commonly rich in humor, and this form of play with language obviously persists into adulthood. People whose sense of humor remains undeveloped for one reason or another miss out on one of the great pleasures of life, and one of the great gifts of the tool kit of language.

Jokes help to draw attention to the distance between what language can establish and the reality that can never be adequately captured in it. The joke seems to be a universal consequence of language development, and as such we ignore its role in teaching at our peril. It is noteworthy, in this context, to repeat Steven Pinker's observation: "Metaphor and humor are useful ways to summarize the two mental performances that go into understanding a sentence" (1994, p. 230).

Joking, again, might seem to have little central place in learning—perhaps a frill or entertaining feature for those with a taste for it, and the hard work of learning might use humor only as a *hook*, a device to get students' attention so the real work can begin. But this imaginative approach to teaching elevates humor from some occasional side-player to one of the heavy lifters of enlarged understanding.

It may seem that using humor and jokes is a personal decision of the teacher, dependent on a taste for it or on a personality trait. But I think this is to trivialize one of the most powerful techniques we have for understanding. The joke is commonly based on incongruity—looking at one thing in so obviously the wrong context or category that it helps to reinforce the category it pretends to disrupt. Well, one needn't get bogged down in the analysis of the joke to recognize something oddly comic about human attempts to understand the world around us. We bring such pitiful equipment to the task. We were designed to live in groups, find food, procreate, and die, and here we are trying to grasp the stars and fit the universe into the categories of our cognition. Not exactly futile, but good that children learn something about the cosmic dimension of the comedy of learning about the world as well as learning the peculiar trick of making a part of our thinking external to our bodies, and taking into our minds the thoughts of others perhaps long dead.

In the imaginative classroom, then, we will expect to see much more humor than is currently common. Rather than suppressing jokes about the topic at hand, teachers will encourage students to generate good jokes—quite quickly the mindless wisecrack will be seen to represent only a failure of imagination, and genuine wit will be encouraged. At least, that's been the common experience. Math, for example, though I suppose no differently from all areas of the curriculum, is alive with endless possibilities for humor. With early counting one can ask the students, "Why is 6 afraid of 7?" "Because 7, 8, 9." (Seven ate nine. OK, you got it the first time.) "What goes

99 thump, 99 thump, 99 thump. . . ." "A centipede with a wooden leg." "Why is 2 times 10 the same as 2 times 11?" "Because 2 times 10 equals 20, and 2 times 11 equals twenty, too" (22).

Mental Imagery

With the development of oral language came the curious discovery that words could be used to generate images in the mind. These mental images, if we reflect on them, are unlike anything we are familiar with in the world. We use the perhaps slightly misleading word *image* for them, because some quasi-pictorial mental images do seem like pictures—so much so that we can scan them with closed eyes as though we are looking at a scene in reality (Shepard, 1975). But many of the images we generate in our minds are of things that have no visual analog; we can, for example, evoke the "image" of a smell.

Because of the importance in oral cultures of preserving information in the memory, all cognitive tools were bent to support this socially vital activity. So we find myths, for example, full of vivid and bizarre images. As has been evident for a long time, the more exotic, surprising, or strange the image that we form, the more memorable it is.

Perhaps I might interrupt this narrative to mention that I have a friend who owns a farm northwest of Kalgoorlie in Western Australia. On the west and south sides of the house there is a wide verandah whose floor is made of red jarrah wood, on which one is expected to walk barefoot—a cool pleasure in the warm days. There is a lawn of rough grass that falls away down to a small river. In the curve of the river around the house, a former owner planted seven jacaranda trees. On a recent visit we sat on the verandah each late afternoon, shaded by the huge canopies of the purple-flowered jacarandas, and discussed our day's work to the sound of the pebbled river and the wind through the scented trees.

Sorry—I lied. I don't have a friend with a farm northwest of Kalgoorlie. I've never been there. But anyone can spend only about two and a half minutes scribbling such an invention and, if one does it even marginally well, it can generate an image in the reader's mind. Many of our narratives do not generate such images; compare this paragraph with the preceding one. Those that do generate images are easier to read and to remember. We would be foolish to ignore this power of language in planning how to teach. The kinds of images we might want to evoke will likely be different in each case, but in both cases the power of language to evoke images provides a cognitive tool of considerable power. Perhaps some day I'll drive up to Kalgoorlie and bemusedly search for a cool verandah of jarrah wood and a stream behind purple-flowering jacarandas. Perhaps you might too?

We can often recall images from stories told to us in our earliest years. Curiously, the images we formed as we listened to the stories are often more vivid in our memories than pictures in books. (I offer this observation tentatively; it is based only on my informal surveys of around twenty adults over the past couple of years. But the uniform results are suggestive at least. And nearly everyone who sees a movie after having read the original book claims to be disappointed. One of the few exceptions I am aware of is the *Lord of the Rings* set, and in this case immense amounts of money were spent on simulating the images Tolkien himself had left behind.) Sinbad's cave or Mowgli's jungle remain not simply as vivid quasi-pictorial images; they are also repositories of emotions and can evoke immensely powerful nostalgic feelings. That is, the images come along with an emotional coloring. So we can manage to both think and feel in terms of the common images we can evoke in our minds.

In teaching, we tend to focus our attention on the content or skills we want the learner to grasp. Often we will consider the basic concepts we want to communicate. Rarely, in my experience and from my reading of teacher-education methods texts, do we reflect on the vivid images that might be evoked by the content we wish to teach. Given the universality of image-generation in all oral cultures, it would be prudent to reflect on ways to use this cognitive tool in teaching. We may be sure learners have the power to generate mental images, and might easily and pleasurably exercise this power.

In the imaginative classroom we will see much greater invocation of images in all curriculum areas. In teaching about place value or decimalization in math, for example, instead of the usual explanation of the principle and then much drill, practice, and repetition, the teacher will pause in planning the lesson and think what image might help students' imaginative engagement with the topic and their understanding of it. So we can imagine a king who wants to count his army. A clever councilor suggests that the king have five servants pick up ten stones each, then stand behind a table. In front of each servant on the table is a bowl. The army then marches by the end of the table, and the servant at the end puts a stone into his bowl for each soldier who marches past. When the ten are down, he picks them up, and continues putting one in his bowl for each passing soldier. The servant to his left watches him and each time he picks up his ten stones, she puts one down. When her ten are in the bowl, she picks them out and continues putting one stone in the bowl each time the servant to her right picks up his ten stones. The third servant simply watches the second servant, and each time she picks up her ten stones, he puts one into his bowl. And so it goes, with the servant to the far left having a very dull time waiting for the servant to his right to pick up her ten stones. After some hours, the servant at the far left has one stone in his bowl, the next servant has three stones in her bowl, the next servant has two stones in his bowl, the next servant has no stones in her bowl, and the servant at the end of the table—exhausted after the hardest day's work—has nine stones in his bowl. The clever councilor is able to tell the king that he has thirteen thousand two hundred and nine soldiers in the army. The drill and practice that follows such an image might involve the students counting themselves or other objects using such a method. It need not displace other techniques for teaching about place value and decimalization, but it does tend to make the topic vividly clear to students, and meaningful, and imaginatively engaging.

Gossip

Gossip has come, disparagingly, to mean idle chatter or even malicious rumor-mongering, talk of no social importance or seriousness. Gossip, as a result of old and discredited prejudices, was associated generally with the casual talk of women, talk usually focused on matters of the home and family and local events rather then the "important" (that is, male) areas of business and politics, generally distinguishing between talk belonging to the private rather than public world. The word, in English, comes from *godsibb,* a person related to one in God, as in *godparent,* and gossip is the kind of talk we might have with such a person.

Anthropologists increasingly recognize in gossip one of the most important sources of human social stability, and see it also as perhaps the arena for the first development of language (Mithen, 1996, chapter 10). It is not insignificant that this form of talk about everyday social activity is usually the easiest for us, and the form that we (whether male or female) engage in most readily (Dunbar, 1991). Gossip narratives are, of course, a kind of story, so this cognitive tool has features in common with the earlier discussion of the story form. But gossip is also different in its informality, its casualness, its common lack of formal structuring.

I was at a conference recently and a graduate student from a different university told me that the interesting paper we had just heard by the well-known Professor X was actually her work! She had written an assignment for his course, for which he had given her only a B, and then he had presented her paper almost unchanged as his own. He gave himself away because he quoted Foucault in his paper, as she had done, but included as a part of the supposed Foucault quote her following discussion of it! As we drank our beer, she said she was as angry with herself as with him. She should have stood up and told everyone he had stolen her work. But she worried that no one would believe her. She also worried that she would have to ask him for references for job applications in a few months, and her career could depend on his willingness to write them.

Yes, sorry, I'm making all this up too. (Though, I fear, this is an invention with too many real analogs.) Was the paragraph easier to read than the one that preceded it?

The capacity to gossip entails the narratizing of events, coloring our representation of events with appropriately recognized emotion, organizing events by identifying acceptable causal sequences, integrating motives into the causal sequences, interpreting intentions in diverse personalities, and so on. These are, needless to say, enormously sophisticated cognitive capacities. But we can be confident that our students already have developed these tools in significant degree.

While we think of gossip as idle or time-wasting, it does, of course, continue to play a vital social role. It represents perhaps the oldest of the cognitive tools of orality. In teaching students who will have the tools of orality in place, then, we will want to reflect on how we might build on those capacities we can see and enjoy vividly in gossip.

In the imaginative classroom we will expect to see much readier use of gossip than is common at present, at least in the classrooms I have seen. All teachers know that if they pause and tell the students about some weird event or accident that they saw on the way to school, attention is immediately enhanced; if the event is well told, one can feel the intensity of interest among the students. The trick is to think about whatever topic one is teaching, and introduce items of gossip that will enhance understanding and engage students' imaginations. The lives of mathematicians, scientists, explorers, and writers are chock-full of incidents that are not the usual focus of teaching, but that can enlighten and enliven a great deal of the world students are learning about.

It seems too little recognized that good literacy skills rely heavily on the development of good orality skills. While young children live in an oral culture, it is too often the case that their oral cognitive tools are not adequately developed. What many students who are having difficulty with literacy need is a richer orality to build literacy on. Commonly in schools, students who have difficulties reading and writing are seated by themselves in front of a computer or with worksheets, cutting them off from the oral development that they most precisely need. And at home they may spend hours in front of TV or playing with electronic gadgets, all of which do nothing to develop the cognitive tools that are most needed. Gossip in early childhood is one of the easiest ways to develop the foundations for rich orality on which we can then build a rich literacy. Good literacy skills rely heavily on the development of good orality skills.

Play

Endless books and articles deal with the importance of play, so I don't need to repeat the wisdom about its educational uses you will find better expressed elsewhere. Briefly, though, in terms of cognitive tools, play can develop a wide array of symbolic functions. Perhaps most useful, continuing the discussion of gossip, are those fantasy games children elaborate themselves: taking roles, spinning imaginary worlds, gossiping endlessly as they do so, making contractual arrangements about rules, and just having a really good time. One crucial value of play is the way it releases the mind to reflect back on the world. Again, it is a tool that develops that metalevel of thinking; it helps us to think about the world in a way freed from the constraints that the world's normal forms, behavior, and everyday purposes impose on us.

In play we also learn crucial capacities of self-control. Having taken on a role, we cannot respond except in that role. If we are playing a witch, we have to do evil, while at the same time recognizing it as evil. The subtlety and variety of developments that can take place as a result of giving much opportunity for play need no elaboration here. It is a cognitive tool of immense value and varied forms.

In Vygotsky's view, play commonly generates a "zone of proximal development" that draws the child on to develop higher levels of psychological functioning improving memory, language, empathy, and reasoning. Vygotsky argued that, in play, children function beyond their average abilities as indicated by routine everyday activities. Play provides a great experimental situation in which children explore the rules of their society and culture (1978).

Electronic "play," which is working hard (to some people's profit) to disrupt this immensely valuable negotiated play among children, has been described as "fast food for the imagination."

Overindulged—which doesn't take much—it has similar effects on the arteries of the imagination.

In the imaginative classroom we will expect to see much more play than is currently common. The kind of play, whether board game, inventive, competitive, exploratory, puzzle-based, or whatever, will depend a lot on the topic being taught. In our experience with "imaginative education," we have found that use of these tools tends to lead to creating situations in the classroom where children take roles in units. So, if teaching about the Properties of the Air, the children can be divided into groups in which they explore the behavior of radio waves, or fly-poop, or muons, or pollen, but, in doing so, they take on the role of these entities, and have to interact with others appropriately. In the conclusion of the unit, they can construct hugely magnified models of the entities they represent. Or they can play the king and his councilors in learning about Place Value, some playing the role of soldiers. Virtually every topic in the curriculum can be conceived in such a way that children can be given roles to play and so explore the topic with greater intensity and engagement.

The Recognition of Mystery

I recognize that there is some risk in including *mystery* on this list of cognitive tools. Apart from any other reason, it might seem just plain odd to call the recognition of mystery a "cognitive tool." There is also a problem with the popular sensationalism that is associated with the use of the word, as in "mysteries of the Bermuda triangle" or "mysteries of the ancient world," though perhaps less objectionable is "mysteries of nature." But I think we can see ways in which a sense of the mystery of things is an important component in the growth of understanding. It is a tool that allows us to recognize that whatever we learn is at best only a tiny fragment of what is to be known. The sense of mystery makes this realization not disabling or depressing but exciting and enticing—drawing the student toward the vast riches of understanding that remain available. So I don't simply want to dismiss that sensational aspect of mystery as it might appear also in the headlines of such publications as the *National Enquirer*, but rather to work out how it may be turned to educational purposes.

Mystery enables the mind increasingly to recognize that the world around us, the world we can see and hear and learn how to behave within, is only the immediate surface under which, or behind which, or beyond which are intellectual riches and experiences barely guessed. Mystery is our sense that there is more than we can see and hear and experience in our environment. By opening our minds to this wider, stranger, and less easily accessible world, we create the first tool for its exploration. I suppose poets have best expressed this drive to go beyond the routine. In Tennyson's words:

> *Yet all experience is an arch wherethro'*
> *Gleams that untravell'd world whose margin fades*
> *For ever and forever when I move.*
> *To follow knowledge like a sinking star,*
> *Beyond the utmost bound of human thought.*
>
> —From "Ulysses"

Mind you, Tennyson got it from Dante, whose Ulysses described his desire to:

> *. . . shrink not from new experience;*
> *But sailing still against the setting sun,*
> *Seek we new worlds where Man has never won*
> *Before us. Ponder your proud destinies:*
> *Born were ye not like brutes for swinish ease,*
> *But virtue and high knowledge to pursue.*
>
> —From *Inferno*, Canto XXVI

At one level the sense of mystery is a part of developing intellectual humility. One of the best-known expressions of this came from perhaps the greatest scientific mind of all time. Sir Isaac New-ton (1642–1727) wrote to his nephew that while people might think him so knowledgeable as a result of his work in mathematics, optics, physics, and astronomy, and his discovery of the law of grav-itation, the formulation of the basic laws of motion, the develop-ment of the calculus, and the analysis of the nature of white light, and so on, he himself took the opposing view: "I seem to have been only like a boy playing on the seashore, and diverting myself in now and then finding a smoother pebble or a prettier shell than ordinary, whilst the great ocean of truth lay all undiscovered before me" (quoted in David Brewster, 1965 [1855]).

Well, I've pulled in some heavy lifters to help me describe this tool. Drawing on poets indicates something of the difficulty of char-acterizing the capacity to recognize the mystery of things as a cog-nitive tool, but I hope it will become clearer from the examples to come. It seems fair to say that behind every explanation lies a mys-tery. It seems so fair to say it that I'm sure someone must already have done so.

In the imaginative classroom we will expect to see much greater emphasis on mysteries. These can indeed involve the more sensational kinds trumpeted by popular papers, but should also move constantly in the direction of the deeper mysteries be-yond our range of knowledge. Even with simple counting, the idea of infinity can be brought forward for quite young children to butt their heads against. When learning about prime numbers, students can be invited to find some pattern in the appearance of primes, and then can be told that this is one of the most persis-tent puzzles mathematicians have grappled with unsuccessfully for centuries. Punctuation, such as the ingenious comma, can lead to students' being invited not just to learn the rules but to wonder about how these various squiggles make the page more hospitable to the eye, and they could be invited to invent new punctuation marks that would add to the courtesy that is the heart of punctuation. These different ways of seeing the familiar constantly open up mysteries surrounding our small and insecure space of knowledge.

Embryonic Tools of Literacy

Increasingly, as students become competent in using the general tool kit of language in its many forms, and become increasingly competent readers and writers, teachers might want to begin incorporating into their planning and teaching some of the cognitive tools of the literacy tool kit—especially the use of the extremes of experience, the limits of reality, and the adventures of heroes, and the sense of wonder drawn from narrative understanding and the literate eye.

In the imaginative classroom we can expect a recognition of the changes that are going on in students' understanding with the growth of literacy. I explore these in Chapter Two, but at a general level it is clear that the shift to literacy reflects also a shift from a dominance of the ear to the eye in gathering information. Certain activities can facilitate this shift and also show students how literacy can give new powers. One of the most basic of these activities can be demonstrated through the making and manipulation of lists, and of flowcharts, diagrams, and so on. These are tools unavailable in oral societies, except in restricted forms. But students becoming literate can get great pleasure and imaginative stimulation from making lists and manipulating them. They might be invited, for example, to use an atlas and make a list of rivers, then they can be asked to classify them in tables that might include such categories as "those that are more than 500 miles long," "those that flow through more than one country," "those that are named after a person," and so on. Or they might make a list of the sports they know, and then classify them into sublists of "those in which we kick a ball," "those in which we hit a ball with something," "those in which the goal is off the ground," "those we play indoors," "those in which more than two teams compete," "those that can only be played by two people," and so on.

◆

In the overview near the beginning of this chapter I introduced the cognitive tools I would be telling you about, then I told you about them, so now it's time to tell you what I told you.

The underlying theory is that we can make the best sense of education and students' learning if we think of these processes in terms of the cognitive tools students have to learn with (Egan, 1997). In this chapter I have made a kind of inventory of some of the chief tools young children will normally have available to make sense of the curriculum. Some of these will already be familiar in one form or another, such as the use of stories or humor, but as a set they will perhaps seem a little unusual. This is not the way teachers have been encouraged to think of children's learning, and these are not the focus of much attention when it comes to describing methods of planning and teaching in pre-service education programs.

Despite their unfamiliarity, I hope that even from a brief description of each, it may be evident how some of them can be used for educational purposes. As you read, I hope it will become increasingly clear that, in fact, focusing on these kinds of cognitive tools is precisely what's needed to engage students' imaginations in learning. The tools are not to be seen as some kinds of hooks or motivators. They are clues to help solve the problem of how to make knowledge about the world meaningful to the students. Engaging the imagination is not a sugar-coated adjunct to learning; it is the very heart of learning. It is what brings meaning and sense and context and understanding to the knowledge we wish to teach.

*Engaging the imagination is not a sugar-coated
adjunct to learning; it is the very heart of learning.*

So what I've told you about—stories, metaphors, binary opposites, rhyme and rhythm and pattern, jokes and humor, mental imagery, gossip, play, and mystery—are among the first important keys to some of those doors to our culture's riches, a set of auxiliary tools that fit onto the great tool of language itself. We will not simply be exploiting these tools, we will be exercising and developing them at the same time, because these are the tools of our early understanding.

What remains is to show how focusing on such characteristics of students' minds can actually lead to new and effective ways of planning and teaching. My initial plan had been to describe the sets of cognitive tools that come with language, then those that come with literacy, then those that come with theoretic thinking, and then give examples. But increasingly it seems like too long a haul through descriptions of sets of cognitive tools before getting to some account of how the tools might be used. So I thought I'd add an in-between chapter after each descriptive chapter in order to give some flavor of how the tools might be used to shape teaching and learning.

In Chapter Two I look at a new set of cognitive tools that are a part of literacy's tool kit. The set presented so far don't simply go away as the new ones develop, however. They blend in some cases and continue to develop in distinctive ways in others. Stories, for example, may change into more sophisticated narratives—but simpler stories continue to engage more sophisticated students and adults. The capacities for metaphor and mental imagery continue to develop. I don't pursue some of these in much detail, but I just want to note that the cognitive tools and their associated capacities that people learn early in life are not abandoned with the acquisition of additional tools. Neither are they unchanged by further growth, but they also remain available in their simpler forms as well. A bit complicated, but that's the trouble with being human. While simple theories of development are attractive, it's hard to take them seriously when one looks at the messy complexity of the world and its people.

Examples in Everyday Classrooms

The purpose here is to explore various ways in which the principles and cognitive tools described in Chapter One can be used in everyday practice. I gave some suggestions about the use of individual tools in the classroom as I described them, but here I want to explore how using them all together can reshape teachers' approaches to everyday teaching.

The cognitive tools discussed in Chapter One fit together into a planning framework. Please forgive the apparent metaphoric confusion here—child's play to a five-year-old!—and see what I mean by using the tools *as parts of the framework* and not just as a way to build a framework. The trick is to pull together all the ideas, principles, and cognitive tools into a format that will help you plan imaginative lessons and units.

At first look, no doubt, the frameworks will appear a bit odd—they don't fit the more common "Objectives / Content / Methods / Evaluation" techniques derived from Ralph Tyler's work (1949), which are still taught in most pre-service teacher education programs. Instead, they are designed as a kind of crutch to help teachers lay out a lesson plan or a unit of study for imaginatively engaging students using the set of cognitive tools described earlier. My expectation is that while these frameworks may be useful for the first few tries at planning such a lesson, teachers will leave them behind and incorporate the elements they find useful into their regular practice, perhaps finding the descriptions useful later as a reference or reminder as well.

You can imagine that over some years of working with many teachers these frameworks have changed and developed. I think the basic structure has remained fairly constant, but it has grown more elaborate through the years. So here I begin with the simplest skeleton framework and give a couple of examples of using it, then move on to a more developed version that builds more support into the process of planning. The first couple of examples are just designed to show in general how using the basic framework would affect teaching a particular topic, then I move on to explore further possibilities in the more elaborated form. I also give examples of various kinds of topics, from fairly easy ones (in the sense that their imaginative possibilities are relatively easy to see—like the growth of a butterfly from an egg to a larva to a pupa)—to more difficult ones (in the sense that it is far from obvious how to engage students' imaginations in them—place value in math, or remembering when to use "their," "there," or "they're").

The examples are relatively brief—I've had to fight the temptation to fill pages with support material and suggestions for activities. I will ask you to use your own experience and skill to see the many ways these plans could be fleshed out. (You will also find additional support materials on the Imaginative Education Research Group (IERG) Web site, www.ierg.net.) My purpose here is to show the frameworks' impact on everyday curriculum content and not to replicate the many excellent books about particular activities that can be used—though I do make some suggestions along these lines here and there.

The Simple Version

So here is the simplest version of the framework:

First Planning Framework (Simple Version)

1. *Identifying importance:* What is most important about this topic? Why should it matter to the students? What is emotionally engaging about it?

2. *Finding binary opposites:* What binary opposites best show the importance of the topic?
3. *Organizing content in story form:*
    3.1. What content can show the importance of the binary opposites in order to provide clear access to the topic?
    3.2. What content best shapes the topic into a developing story form?
4. *Conclusion:* What is the best way of resolving the dramatic conflict inherent in the binary opposites? What degree of mediation of those opposites is it appropriate to seek?
5. *Evaluation:* How can we know whether the topic has been understood, its importance grasped, and the content learned?

Example One: Place Value

How can we use this framework to make a lesson about place value and decimalization in math imaginatively engaging to a typical second-grade class? Here is the original example I designed to show how this framework could be of some help to teachers.

The first task is find something important and emotionally engaging about the topic. This might seem a peculiar place to start: emotional engagement with place value!? This is a way of thinking about teaching that is rarely encouraged, and yet I think every good teacher intuitively does something like this. In this approach, it is the first and most important task of planning, and sometimes the hardest.

Perhaps I should emphasize that what is being suggested here is rather different from the common idea of looking for a hook to catch students' interest. While that can be of some use in engaging students' imaginations, the task here is rather to take an overview of the topic and think about why it is important to students, important not just in the practical sense but for enriching or enlarging their understanding and appreciation of the world.

The following sections take the steps from the model and show how they can give shape and life to a lesson:

1. Identifying Importance. *What is most important about this topic? Why should it matter to the students? What is emotionally engaging about it?*

The model begins with a request to locate the importance of the topic of place value, with the expectation that whatever is identified will have some emotional resonance. It is tempting to answer the question about why it matters in utilitarian terms: "Math is of practical value to any person today, and so learning about place value is important for the students because they will make constant errors in calculating their finances if they don't understand it." And, indeed, that will have to be part of the answer, but it is a way of thinking about the topic in a purely mechanical way and ignoring the emotional importance it can have to students and, perhaps more important at this point, to us the teachers. That is, if we can't find anything in the topic that engages us emotionally, we are unlikely to be able to engage the students in it.

What you have to capture is something of the incredible ingenuity built into the place value system. Often the trick is bringing out something people commonly take so much for granted that they don't even notice it. For the student, if we teach the concept as necessary to learn simply because it is of practical use to be able to do more math in the future, we can too easily make it appear dull. Students can be persuaded quite easily to take wonders for granted too, unless we help them identify what is wonderful about a topic. So you can identify the wonderful *ingenuity* of place value as what is important, why it should matter, and what can be emotionally engaging about the topic.

2. Finding Binary Opposites. *What binary opposites best show the importance of the topic?*

If the quality identified as important is ingenuity, then you might build your unit on the opposition between ingenuity and cluelessness, or you could frame it as between imaginativeness and unimaginativeness.

3. *Organizing Content in Story Form.* This point has two subsidiary questions: *What content can show the importance of the binary opposites in order to provide clear access to the topic?* and *What content can shape the topic into a developing story form?*

Now I need first to emphasize again that the term *story form* doesn't mean that you have to make your lessons and units into fictional stories, nor that you need to tell fictional stories as a part of your lessons and units. Teachers can use this framework without ever using any fictional story at all—in the sense that the newspaper editor calling for a story on the downtown fire is not asking a reporter to make something up. But, having emphasized that, there is also no reason not to use a fictional story to teach a topic if one will do the job. So I'll use fiction for this example, and for Example Two I'll show how to use nonfiction as a "story."

So the first teaching task needs to be one that exposes the contrast between ingenuity and cluelessness in such a way that the sheer cleverness of the decimal system is made clear to the students. One way to do this is to contrast it to ways in which nondecimal systems work and also, more basically, how a decimal system differs from using our natural number sense.

I sometimes begin teaching this topic by telling the story of the crow and the farmer: a story you may know.

> The farmer has a huge old barn in which he keeps his grain, but the barn has holes and gaps all over it. A fat crow comes daily and squeezes into the barn and eats the grain. The farmer becomes obsessed with this crow, and determines to shoot it. But every time he leaves the farmhouse to go out to the barn, the crow hears the door open and flies away. The crow then sits on a distant tree. The farmer tries waiting in the barn with his gun till the crow comes back. However long the farmer waits, the crow doesn't return. But as soon as the farmer returns to the farmhouse, the crow flies back and sets about eating the grain again. Then the farmer has an idea. The next day he takes a friend with him into the barn. As soon as the two of

them emerge from the house, the crow flies away as usual. But after about ten minutes in the barn, the friend leaves, slams the barn door, goes into the farmhouse and slams its door, and the farmer waits in the barn with his gun for the crow to return. The crow doesn't return. Eventually the farmer gives up and heads for the farmhouse. As soon as he goes in, the crow flies back and eats the grain. The next day the farmer takes two friends into the barn. After a while the two friends return to the farmhouse, and the farmer waits in the barn with his gun, but the crow doesn't return until the farmer also goes into the farmhouse. The next day, the farmer takes three friends with him to the barn, with the same results. The next day, four friends, and still no luck. By the end of the week, the farmer and his *seven* patient friends go into the barn. The seven friends leave and go into the farmhouse. The farmer waits in the barn as usual, and the crow flies back to the barn, and the farmer shoots it!

What a terrible story! The point of the story is that blackbirds have a number sense of about seven, which is the same as human beings have. This story, which might take about three or four minutes to tell (depending on how much drama a teacher wants to add!), introduces the importance of counting systems. If we rely on a number sense that doesn't work with any precision above seven, we might find ourselves getting shot like the crow. The cleverness of counting enables us to do all kinds of things, and to deal with very large numbers with precision.

Having indicated something of the ingenuity of counting with one story, we might move to another in order to shape the content into an emotionally engaging form. Here's a somewhat more elaborate version of the soldier-counting tale from Chapter One:

Let us imagine a king who wants to count his army, but the councilors he asks can't come up with a simple way to do it. One suggests marking sticks, cutting a notch for each soldier, another suggests some way of matching them with fixed objects they could then count, and some said that "very many" was the number of the soldiers. None of the councilors seemed able to devise a good system for counting them. At this point the king turns to his daughter in despair because he knows she is clever. She says she can tell him how many soldiers there are. First, she tells each of the five clueless councilors to pick up ten stones each. Then she has a table laid in the field to which the soldiers will be marching from their tents. The clueless councilors are asked to stand in line behind the table, and then a bowl is placed in front of each of them.

As the soldiers go by, the councilor at the end of the table puts a stone in his bowl for each soldier. Once the ten stones have been put into the bowl, he picks them up and carries on putting one stone into his bowl for each soldier who walks past. So he has a rather busy afternoon, putting stones in his bowl as the soldiers go by, and picking them up and starting again on the next ten. The clueless councilor to his left has the less arduous job of watching him put his stones in the bowl, and each time he picks up his ten stones the second clueless councilor puts one stone into his bowl. When the second councilor has put all ten stones in his bowl, he too picks them up again, and continues to put one down each time his fellow councilor picks up his ten. The third clueless councilor has only to watch the bowl of the second, and each time the second councilor picks up his ten stones, the third councilor puts one into his bowl. And so it goes on, with the fifth councilor having a very slow afternoon, putting a stone down when the fourth councilor picks up his ten. At the end of the afternoon, the fifth clueless councilor has one stone in his bowl, the next councilor has seven, the third has none, the second has one, and the first, exhausted, councilor has six. The daughter looks at the bowls and tells the king that he has seventeen thousand and sixteen soldiers in his army.

As stories go, this isn't exactly a thriller, but what it does do is focus on the sheer brilliant ingenuity of the decimal system for keeping count of large numbers of objects and showing students why place value matters. The rest of the lesson, or the next lesson, can involve the students in counting objects using this method.

Two things commonly occur when place value is taught like this. The first is that the students learn the point of decimal systems quickly and well, and understand, for example, why one can't simply ignore a zero in a decimal system. The second thing that usually happens is that the students make an emotional association with the ingenuity of the king's daughter, and so with the ingenuity of the decimal system. They see it as something clever, not something to take for granted. It is wonderful, and that sense of wonder needs to be captured to engage the students with place value.

4. Conclusion. *What is the best way of resolving the dramatic conflict inherent in the binary opposites? What degree of mediation of those opposites is it appropriate to seek?*

How to conclude a lesson like this? It's necessary to somehow resolve or mediate between the ingenuity and cluelessness on which the lesson is built so far. In the conclusion you might ask the students how the king's daughter might have been able to count the army if there had been no stones around. What can they think of that is easily available that might do the job? She could have arranged the councilors so that one raised a finger each time a soldier went by and made a fist to close his fingers when each ten had passed; the next councilor would put up a single finger when the councilor to the right closed his fist, and so on down the line. You might also encourage students to recognize that the ingenuity involved in the first person's invention of a decimal system of counting was stunning, and so they shouldn't really talk of the councilors as clueless—they simply didn't have great imaginations, which is the lot of most of us. But by recognizing and associating with the imaginativeness of the ingenious inventor of decimal counting systems, the students can begin to move a little in the direction of being, or wishing to be, ingenious themselves. It would also be useful to make clear that while this story is a fiction, and the king's daughter imaginary, someone at some time did invent this system. It isn't just a routine bit of another textbook to be taken for granted; it is a product of someone's wonderful ingenuity.

5. Evaluation. *How can we know whether the topic has been under-stood, its importance grasped, and the content learned?*

Any of the usual assessment procedures can be used. In my ex-perience, students whose imaginations have been caught up in a topic do better on all standardized tests of achievement. I think every teacher knows this; the problem has been how to engage imaginations in such topics as place value or punctuation and so on. So there is likely to be no problem using standard tests of content mastery.

But, given the aim of engaging the students' imaginations in learning, you will also want some evidence that you have achieved this too. Various kinds of information, including that derived from discussion, debate, artwork, and journal writing, can be gained as the students apply to a slightly different task the technique demon-strated in the story. Look for such things as emotional engagement, imaginative involvement, and the deployment of the cognitive tools that you have used and wish to develop. What kind of evi-dence could one harness to measure emotional engagement and imaginative involvement and cognitive tool development?

Most experienced teachers would have little difficulty in most cases identifying which students experience these at varying degrees of intensity. The teacher might be alert to such things as the amount of continuous time a student spends engaged in a project developed from the initial story, the kinds of questions and com-ments made, the originality of the student's contributions to the task based on the story, the degree of commitment to the project, the recognition of the role of great ingenuity in the solution the king's daughter came up with and how the students might be trying to reflect this in their own work at an appropriate level, competence and confidence in written, oral, and pictorial presentations, the vividness, originality, and relevance of images used by students in their oral language, in writing, and in pictorial displays. More tra-ditional forms of evaluation and the newer qualitative procedures can be used, of course, to give evidence of the degree and extent of children's knowledge of the content.

Now obviously no teacher will be deploying this panoply of evaluation procedures for each lesson. I just wanted to indicate that there are things to look at that will give some index of how well the unit might be engaging students' imaginations, as well as teaching them the content. There are also a range of dynamic assessment devices that you can use, derived from Vygotsky's work, and available on the www.ierg.net Web site.

(*Note:* Tannis Calder has written a more elaborate—and much better—story treatment of this concept, "Mita and the Ograk," available at www.ierg.net. In this version, a young girl saves her village from a monster by using a small number of objects and her pockets to precisely count large numbers.)

Example Two: Butterfly Transformations

Here's an "easy" topic—the one about the butterfly—to illustrate how you can use the framework to shape facts into a (nonfictional) story form.

The transformations the butterfly goes through before reaching its familiar state as a glorious flying flower have enough drama that it doesn't take much work to make the topic engaging to students' imaginations. It might be worth running quickly through the framework, to see how it would suggest a particular shape for a unit on butterfly transformations. I won't go into the various activities that you might use with students, as these will be fairly familiar, and there are endless resources to support such a unit. My only concern here is with how to shape it to bring out the imagination-engaging drama that is so readily apparent in the topic.

1. Identifying Importance. *What is most important about this topic? Why should it matter to the students? What is emotionally engaging about it?*

Stop and think about just what it is about the butterfly's transformations that are important and emotionally engaging. The life cycle of the butterfly demonstrates something almost unique in the degree of transformation it goes through. It is a study in oppositions:

from the caterpillar that does almost nothing but eat to the butterfly that eats nothing, only sips nectar; from the dull, narrow chrysalis to the bright-winged jewel of the air; from the largely immobile caterpillar to the butterfly that sometimes migrates more than a thousand miles; from the incessantly growing caterpillar to the butterfly that is unchanging after it emerges from the chrysalis, and so on. Most creatures, including ourselves, go through dramatic changes as we age, but virtually nothing else changes so astonishingly. Knowledge about the butterfly gives us a vivid insight into the wonder of the forms of life on our planet.

2. Finding Binary Opposites. *What binary opposites best show the importance of the topic?*

What abstract, emotional opposite concepts might we use to build the knowledge on? One possible set is constrained/free. The story of the unit, in this case, will be how butterflies become able to fly free in the air having been constrained in one place on the ground. (It would be possible to choose other oppositions; the choices would dictate somewhat different story lines, even though the knowledge to be taught would remain much the same. Alternatives that would refocus the lesson would be little change/dramatic change, voracious/abstemious, or even ugly/beautiful.)

3. Organizing Content in Story Form. *What content can show the importance of the binary opposites in order to provide clear access to the topic?* and *What content can shape the topic into a developing story form?*

You might begin with butterfly eggs, tiny and still, giving no hint of what they will become. Then you can tell students that within the prisons of the shells the creatures are preparing for a great escape, but to achieve this they will need to transform themselves a number of times; they face a series of constraints preventing them from being free. The tiny caterpillars emerge, eating their way out, then they eat the rest of the shell, and then they continue to eat, eat, eat. They are among the most single-minded and voracious eaters in the animal world, growing till they burst their skins, molting, then eating, eating till they burst their skins again. All this eating is a preparation for their escape. How? How can growing bigger and bigger enable them to escape from the leaves they never move from, and move *on* only to find new things to eat? They consume hundreds of times their body weight, in some species thousands of times. They are mostly just jaws, claws, claspers, and a digestive system. Greatly enlarged photographs expose them as fearsome, ugly monsters.

But then, quite suddenly, they stop eating. They molt from their skins one last time and build chrysalises around themselves, in which they lie inert, helpless, and cold. How can they be escaping in there? They are certainly changing again. We can see the hardened chrysalis begin to take the imprint of a developing head, thorax, and legs. But whatever is happening, it does not look like an escape from the prison of the chrysalis.

In the observations and activities the children are involved in so far, it will be important to the story line to emphasize the constrainedness of the caterpillars and chrysalises. Their range of activities and movement is very little, they can't get far at best, they are tied to their food source and then to their chrysalises, they are monochrome and sluggish and a bit dreary. This emphasis needs to be tied to the tension and puzzle of how they are going to be able to escape.

Then the chrysalises are forced slowly apart. What freedom can the caterpillars expect to achieve once they come out? But out comes the first changed head and then a trembling creature with crumpled wings. A rush of blood through the frail body and the wings unfurl, and then sway and flap, and its colors glisten. And it can fly, immediately. The frail butterfly can often migrate over a thousand miles. Even though it can no longer eat, it returns to lay its eggs close to a food source, so the voracious, constrained caterpillars that emerge can set about preparing themselves in turn for the unsuspected winged freedom of the butterfly.

While the information about butterfly transformations will not be different from usual in this lesson, what is different here is the story shape in which we see each change as part of the drama of striving for freedom from the constraints of the earlier forms of egg, caterpillar, and chrysalis. The dramatic changes take on a further meaning within the story.

4. Conclusion. *What is the best way of resolving the dramatic conflict inherent in the binary opposites? What degree of mediation of those opposites is it appropriate to seek?*

You want to show how the opposition between constraint and freedom in the life cycle of the butterfly can be seen as a complex relationship. The ultimate great freedom of the butterfly to travel hundreds of miles is possible only because of the constraint of its earlier forms. The squirrel that can run about very soon after birth usually spends its whole life running about in much the same way over the same territory. By contrast, the early part of the butterfly's life is static and constrained, but that is preparation for a freedom of movement the squirrel will never know. That is, you might conclude this brief unit by looking at the relationship between early constraint and freedom in the lives of other creatures, and compare them with the butterfly's.

5. Evaluation. *How can we know whether the topic has been understood, its importance grasped, and the content learned?*

Any of the usual assessment procedures can be used. The comments made under Example 1 fit equally well here.

Adding Depth to the Framework

Let me now move to a more elaborate version of the framework. This is designed to offer more help to the teacher in the process of constructing the unit or lesson. You will see that some features have been changed from the simple form. Rather than suggest there is some right way to use these cognitive tools, the differences help to indicate that anyone is welcome to come up with their own framework based on the principles and cognitive tools described here.

There is nothing special about the way members of the Imaginative Education Research Group have done it. Here's a skeletal version of this more elaborate form of the first planning framework:

First Planning Framework (More Supportive Version)

1. *Locating emotional meaning:* What is emotionally engaging about this topic? How can it evoke wonder? Why should it matter to us?
2. *Thinking about the content in story form:* How can we shape the content so that it will have some emotional meaning? How can we best bring out that emotional meaning in a way that will engage the imagination?
    2.1. *Finding binary opposites:* What binary concepts best capture the wonder and emotion of the topic? If this were a story, what would the opposing forces be?
    2.2. *Finding images, metaphors, and drama:* What parts of the topic most dramatically embody the binary concepts? What image best captures that content and its dramatic contrast? What metaphors can be used to enrich understanding?
3. *Structuring the body of the lesson or unit:* How do we teach the content in a story form? What additional cognitive tools can we use to make the topic more imaginatively engaging to students?
    3.1. *Locating material that can provide opportunities for gossip and play:* What content connected to the topic can help us to enliven and enrich students' understanding by providing some gossip that they can engage in? What aspects of the content can be used for some form of game or fantasy play or role-playing?
    3.2 *Developing embryonic forms of later cognitive tools:* How can we encourage the use of some of the cognitive tools that come along with literacy while teaching the topic?
4. *Conclusion:* What is the best way to conclude the lesson or unit?
    4.1. *Bringing the story to a satisfactory end:* How does the story end? How do we resolve the conflict set up between the binary opposites? How much do we explain to the stu-

dents about the binary oppositions and how explicit should we make them?

4.2. *Suggesting the mystery behind the topic:* How do we give students some sense of the mystery attached to this topic?

5. *Evaluation:* How can we know whether the topic has been understood, its importance grasped, and the content learned?

These questions are both deeper and more numerous than those in the simple version, so it's useful to explore each of them in detail before proceeding to further examples.

1. Locating Emotional Meaning. *What is emotionally engaging about this topic? How can it evoke wonder? Why should it matter to us?*

A sense of wonder and an emotional response to material are important in engaging students' imaginations. To help students connect emotionally to the material, teachers need to first identify their own emotional attachment to it. So this first question asks the teacher to *feel* for what is wonderful about the topic. This can be difficult if the topic is something like the use of the comma! The trick, though, is to try to re-see the topic through the eyes of the child, to catch at what can stimulate the sense of wonder about even the most routine topics. Especially when teachers have been taught to become expert at organizing classroom activities and structuring topics into instructional units, this can be hard. It asks the teacher to do something that is probably quite unfamiliar—to begin by *feeling* about the topic. Try to indicate for any topic you plan to teach what is wonderful about it, what can give a child an emotional engagement to it.

Things to List:

- Sources of wonder:
- Sources of emotional engagement:

---

2. *Thinking About the Content in Story Form.* *How can we shape the content so that it will have some emotional meaning? How can we best bring out that emotional meaning in a way that will engage the imagination?*

These questions lead in several directions.

2.1. Finding Binary Opposites. What binary concepts best capture the wonder and emotion of the topic? If this were a story, what would the opposing forces be?

Now to the work of locating the best binary oppositions on which to construct the "story" you are going to tell. It should be possible to select the one that seems best, though you might want to note some alternatives, in case the first set doesn't quite carry you through the lesson or unit as well as you expected.

Things to List:

- Main opposition:
- Possible alternative:

2.2. Finding Images, Metaphors, and Drama. What parts of the topic most dramatically embody the binary concepts? What image best captures that content and its dramatic contrast? What metaphors can be used to enrich understanding?

Here the goal is to identify the drama inherent in the topic. Remember, every topic has some kind of dramatic conflict in it. Which conflict best illustrates the binary opposites identified here? Again, for the teacher, trying to *feel* the drama is as important as thinking about it. This task, too, can be quite difficult at first. (It does become easier as you begin to recognize that there is something almost natural about thinking in these terms.) The drama of commas may not be so obvious, nor how one might break up lessons about commas into binary opposites. But everything has within it something dramatic, and everything can be broken down into binary opposites. We are so accustomed to thinking about content, and about concepts, that we often forget that every topic also has a wide range of images attached to it. And the image, remember, can carry the emotional meaning of the topic and can also make the topic much more memorable—if you find a good image, of course. Look for a core conflict, contradiction, or drama that seems to best convey the wonder and emotion of the topic.

Things to List:

- Image or metaphor that captures binary oppositions:
- Content that reflects binary oppositions:

---

3. *Structuring the Body of the Lesson or Unit.* *How do we teach the content in a story form?*

Having done the hard work that has put in place the basic structuring elements—identified the binary opposites and the basic drama—it should be relatively easy to create a narrative plotline of the content. The opposites provide the cognitive and emotional framework of the story. Remember, all good fiction stories are built on a conflict or puzzle; the only difference here is that the "story" content is the curriculum content.

Things to List:

- Overall story structure of the lesson or unit:

3.1 Locating Material That Can Provide Opportunities for Gossip and Play. What content connected to the topic can help us to enliven and enrich students' understanding by providing some gossip that they can engage in? What aspects of the content can be used for some form of game or fantasy play?

Almost any topic includes an opportunity to offer some gossip about characters involved, whether mathematicians, historical characters, scientists, or artists. The teacher can find out some interesting details about their lives, looking especially for anecdotes connected with the topic of the lesson. Sometimes it will be a matter of gossiping about how the knowledge could be used, or in what circumstances it might find some dramatic or amusing application. There are often easily designed games that can help enlarge understanding of some topics, often they might involve role-playing, in which the teacher can also take part. It is sometimes harder to think of ways to encourage fantasy play about a topic, but it isn't as hard as it may initially appear. Guided discovery exercises can be good stimulants to students' own imaginative play with a topic, as they elaborate the images suggested by the teacher's guided discovery narrative.

Things to List:

- Aspects of the topic that might allow opportunities for gossip and play:

3.2. Developing Embryonic Forms of Later Cognitive Tools. How can we encourage the use of some of the cognitive tools that come along with literacy while teaching the topic?

It might seem that this asks too much of the busy teacher, but it often turns out to be surprisingly easy. As you read on and see the set of further cognitive tools, you will see that many of them are already used in greater or lesser degree by many of the students in the earliest grades of schooling. Some teachers find they have an affinity for thinking in terms of some of these later tools and it proves quite easy to build them into some features of a lesson.

Things to List:

- Further cognitive tools that might give shape to the lesson or unit:

---

4. Conclusion. It's still necessary to wrap things up. That process is easier if you ask several specific questions.

4.1. Bringing the Story to a Satisfactory End. How does the story end? How do we resolve the conflict set up between the binary opposites? How much do we explain to the students about the binary oppositions and how explicit should we make them?

Every story has an ending in which the conflict is in some way resolved or at least explained. For younger students a simple resolution may be appropriate; for older students the implications of the opposites and the dramatic space between them can be explored. The conclusion can therefore take on many forms—student presentations, displays, stories that show another form of the opposition being worked out, dramatic presentations of the story with visuals, and so on. Remember, the conclusion is another opportunity for students to feel the drama of the story and internalize the material while expressing their understanding of it in imaginative ways.

Things to List:

- Concluding activity:

4.2. Suggesting the Mystery Behind the Topic. How do we give students some sense of the mystery attached to this topic?

The idea is to enrich and enlarge students' grasp of the topic so they see some sense in which it is mysterious, aiming to create a sense of how much remains to be understood about the topic. One aspect of this can be a fairly everyday sense of how little we actually know, but some aspect must be directed to something more profound about what remains unknown and perhaps unknowable.

Things to List:

- Aspects of the topic that can give students a sense of mystery:

---

5. Evaluation. *How can we know whether the topic has been understood, its importance grasped, and the content learned?*

Any of the traditional forms of evaluation can be used, but in addition, you might want to get some measure of how far students' imaginations have been engaged by the topic. Remember, various kinds of informal evaluations, including discussion, debate, artwork, journal writing, and experiment analysis, can be done while the unit is being taught.

Things to List:

- Forms of evaluation:

Example Three: Properties of the Air

We typically take the air around us for granted. One purpose of this unit is to help students to see that the air is a rich and varied object that they pass through unseeingly all the time. In the classroom in which they sit, the air is more complex and wonderful than almost any of the other objects they attend to.

1. Locating Emotional Meaning. *What is emotionally engaging about the topic? How can it evoke wonder? Why should it matter to us?*

Sources of meaning: An important function of education is to enrich the everyday environment with meaning, uncovering wonder in what is commonly taken for granted. In the case of air, we tend to take it for granted as a kind of emptiness through which we move. This topic should matter to children because it can enlarge and enrich their perception of the world and their understanding of their experience. It can be affectively engaging through its power to evoke, stimulate, and develop the sense of wonder and engage it with reality. It can radically alter their sense of their daily walking and sitting in air.

Sources of emotional engagement: The wonder of the air that they take for granted, and the vast variety of its constituents. We rely on these constituents for life itself, and the array of other living things in the air we breathe is staggering. Any square inch of air contains so many varied materials and life forms that our imaginations can hardly grasp such abundance.

2. Thinking About the Content in Story Form. *How can we shape the content so that it will have some emotional meaning? How can we best bring out that emotional meaning in a way that will engage the imagination?*

2.1. Finding Binary Opposites. What binary concepts best capture the wonder and emotion of the topic? If this were a story, what would the opposing forces be?

Main opposition: One usable binary set for a unit on the properties of the air is empty/full. This may seem a bit simple, with no evident affective "pull." But you can invest emptiness with the affective components of starkness, nothingness, uselessness to life, and fullness with the opposites: varied richness, complexity, and support for life.

Possible alternative: Still/moving.

2.2. Finding Images, Metaphors, and Drama. What parts of the topic most dramatically embody the binary concepts? What image best captures that content and its dramatic contrast?

Image or metaphor that captures the binary oppositions: If possible, darken the room and shine a beam of light through it, catching the inevitable dust. Ask the students what the dust is made up of. Tell them that 60 percent is made up of decayed human skin. Each time they rub their faces or hands together, tiny bits of skin sheer off and then decay, then float on the air. So when we breath in . . . ! Or, if you think it isn't going too far, ask them where they think flies go to the bathroom, and what then happens to fly feces? Well, they too decay and . . . ! Or play a radio in one corner of the room and listen to a voice for a few moments. Then switch it off and go to another corner of the room and change the station to some music. Ask the students how the noises get to the radio. Some will have heard about radio waves. Ask them what the room looks like to a radio; if they had an "eye" like a radio that "sees" radio waves, what would the rest of the room look like? Would it see through walls? Using a metaphor you could suggest that the air is like a tangle of highways through the room for all kinds of strange traffic, some moving super-fast, some dreamily meandering along.

Content that reflects binary oppositions: Start with the sense of the air as being empty and dull, and gradually show that it is in fact the richest, strangest, and most complex thing in the room.

3. *Structuring the Body of the Lesson or Unit.* How do we teach the content in story form?

Overall story structure of the lesson: What's the story about the air? Well, one obvious "story" follows from the fact that we need its gases to be able to live. But how many gases are in the air we breathe? What would the air in the classroom look like if we could see the gases in different colors? And what else is there? Hold out your hand: a million particles from the sun just flashed through it. What are these particles? Are they flowing through us all the time? What is a *muon*? What would the classroom look like if we could see all the atomic and molecular particles passing through it? Why did someone sneeze? Who is allergic to pollens? How many different kinds of pollens might be floating in the air in the room, and how many pollens in all are there in the room? How about viruses and bacteria? What would they look like if we were that size and could see them as big as a person? Are bacteria bigger or smaller than pollens? And what are smells made of? What would the room look like if we could see only smells? Set a fan moving fast—what is moving?

A guided discovery activity could have the students close their eyes and imagine themselves getting smaller and smaller, till they were as tiny as a mote of dust floating in the air of the room. The teacher could then introduce them to various other particles—passing bacteria, Mr. Pollen out for a float—and invite them to be dazzled by the flashing colors of different gases, intersected by endless radio waves passing around them, watch muons and neutrinos zipping by, and so on.

Teachers might introduce lessons on many of the constituents of the air, constantly playing on the contrast with what was thought to be empty and uninteresting, adding one layer of complexity and wonder after another, till the air seems thronged with amazing elements, which we are too gross to notice.

3.1. Locating Material That Can Provide Opportunities for Gossip and Play. *What content connected to the topic can help us enliven and enrich students' understanding by providing some gossip, that they can engage in? What aspects of the content can be used for some form of game or fantasy play?*

Aspects of the topic that might allow opportunities for gossip and play: Teach something about who discovered gases or bacteria, and move beyond birth date and schooling to include some gossipy facts or anecdotes about them. The anecdote could form the basis for a "TV interview," in which one student would interview another who would play the discoverer. Or a student who plays a piece of decayed-skin dust might interview a piece of pollen, and then vice versa. They could discuss where they have been during the day, what made them go from the front of the room to the back, what adventures they had on the way, and what they are doing here in the first place.

3.2. Developing Embryonic Forms of Later Cognitive Tools. *How can we encourage the use of some of the cognitive tools that come along with literacy?*

Further cognitive tools that might give shape to the lesson or unit: Students might be encouraged to explore questions like these: What are the biggest living things that float invisibly in the air and what are the smallest living things? What is the rarest gas present and what is the commonest? What is the most awful smell, and what is it made up of? What happens to the air when it feels hot in a room and when it feels cold? Who discovered about gases and how we need them to live? Who discovered bacteria and why they sometimes make us sick? And similarly for viruses?

4. Conclusion. *What is the best way to conclude the lesson or unit?*

4.1. Bringing the Story to a Satisfactory End. *How does the story end? How do we resolve the conflict set up between the binary opposites? How much do we explain to the students about the binary oppositions and how explicit should we make them?*

Concluding activity: The students could be invited, in small groups, to represent different constituents of the air. Four or five of them might be the pollens, another small group would be radio waves, another dust, another gases, and so on. They would find out, with the teacher's help, as much as possible about their element and then do two things. First, they could make a presentation to the rest of the class about it, but, second, they would construct a model of their element. They might do the presentation while they are building the models. The aim would be to make their models hugely larger than reality, but sized relative to each other, more or less, and in relative quantities to each other. So we might have five large pollen balls and twenty dust chunks. The conclusion of the unit would come with the students' models being hung from the ceiling, perhaps lines of colored threads horizontal from ceiling to floor representing the flashing particles from the sun, and thicker wavy ribbons of many colors coming in various directions representing the radio waves. The final result should give the impression of how crowded with wonders the air is, if only we could see it. The room full of models would suggest what life would be like if people were minute.

4.2. Suggesting the Mystery Behind the Topic. How do we give students some sense of the mystery attached to this topic?

Aspects of the topic that can give students a sense of mystery: If we need oxygen to stay alive and keep breathing it in and using it up, where is all the oxygen coming from? And if plants produce it, how does it all stay in balance: enough oxygen for us and enough carbon dioxide for plants? How thin is the envelope of air around the earth, in which all life lives? Do any other places in the universe have atmospheres like ours? How unusual is earth's development among all the planets in the universe? How can we know? Is there, somewhere in another galaxy now, a small blue plant poking the tips of its leaves through some purple soil? How diverse is life? How rare or common?

5. Evaluation. *How can we know whether the topic has been understood, its importance grasped, and the content learned?*

Forms of evaluation: Any traditional forms of evaluation can be used to assess whether students understand the properties of the air around them. In addition, teachers could assess the degree to which they become knowledgeable in the process of building their models, and can assess their enthusiasm and imaginativeness in doing so. All the comments made in the earlier units under "Evaluation" are also relevant here.

Example Four: Homophones (Knight/Night; Patience/Patients; There/Their/They're)

One of the challenges to teaching spelling in English, and other languages, is the number of words that sound almost alike, or even identical, yet have different spellings and meanings. Here is an approach that can be used to engage children's imaginations while ensuring that children will remember the correct spellings and have some fun in the process. It is a method that can be varied in a number of ways.

1. Locating Emotional Meaning. *What is emotionally engaging about the topic? How can it evoke wonder? Why should it matter to us?*

Sources of meaning: This lesson will evoke wonder concerning the mystery of how sounds convey meaning and the strange ability to derive meaning from arbitrary and abstract symbols.

Sources of emotional engagement: The mystery and wonder that lie at the heart of human language.

2. Thinking About the Content in Story Form. *How can we shape the content so that it will have some emotional meaning? How can we best bring out that emotional meaning in a way that will engage the imagination?*

2.1. Finding Binary Opposites. What binary concepts best capture the wonder and emotion of the topic? If this were a story, what would the opposing forces be?

Main opposition: Meaningful voice/arbitrary symbol.

Possible alternatives: Sound/meaning, same/different.

2.2. Finding Images, Metaphors, and Drama. What parts of the topic most dramatically embody the binary concepts? What image best captures that content and its dramatic contrast?

Image or metaphor that captures the binary oppositions: Returning to the example I used in Chapter One, homophones are like members of a family who have some things in common and some differences. So you could talk about there, their, and they're like family members, with distinctive characters of their own but a very obviously shared common feature. You could imagine that we have these three characters who look alike and are easily confused but who are nevertheless quite distinct individuals. When speaking we never confuse "there" with "their" or with "they're." But when writing, it is easy to confuse them.

Content that reflects binary oppositions: The students need to find a way of distinguishing the spelling just as clearly as they distinguish the meaning of the words when used in oral sentences. The content then will follow from vividly etching the "character" of the written words in the students' minds.

3. Structuring the Body of the Lesson or Unit. *How do we teach the content in story form?*

Overall story structure of the lesson: What's the story on homophones? How can you generate a story context in which the difference between "their," "there," and "they're" will become clear to children?

Each group is given one of the set. Group one gets the girl called "There," group two gets her twin brother "Their," and group three gets their older brother "They're." The groups have to come up with a detailed description of their characters, based on the spelling of the name.

The story developing in this lesson invites the students to generate an image of someone with particular characteristics. The teacher could invite the children to draw their images, indicating in the pictures the features that distinguish "There" from "Their" and "They're."

The teacher could start this off by suggesting that "There" is a very kind and helpful person, whose last three letters seem just to be pointing away to things so people know where they are—she is constantly pointing with the tail of the final "e" that things are there, over there, there. The vowel at the end of the word lets the meaning slide easily out. The first "e" sets up the direction, the "r" checks that that is Right, and the final "e" does the precision pointing. Her character is of a helpful, cheerful, precise person.

"Their" on the other hand is a very egotistical fellow. He is self-regarding—you can tell this because he keeps his ego—his "i"—inside, and traps it with the final consonant. He is also, unfortunately, rather greedy and envious, and constantly goes on about what people own.

You can tell that "They're" is the oldest, as he has grown more letters than the other two. He was always a very inquisitive member of the family, constantly asking "why?" In fact he asked it so often at school that he seemed to have his hand permanently up as soon as he thought of another "y" question to ask, hence the apostrophe. He is a bit boring, as he keeps telling people about what the family is doing or planning all the time: "They're going to get a new car," or "They're going to watch TV tonight," or "They're planning to go to Mexico."

Well, you get the point. The students can work out further elaborations of the characters by observing other features of the words and giving them "personalities."

Having created the characters, the next part of the lesson would be to construct some story in which they take part and in which their particular characters drive the plot. I won't bother working this out here, but you can see how easy it would be to involve the students in constructing a story in which the good-natured "There" is trying to point out where they should go, but the selfish "Their" is concerned that he will lose out on some money if they do, while poor old "They're" is just curious about why they should bother to go there, telling everyone that they're planning to go in the opposite direction next week.

3.1. Locating Material That Can Provide Opportunities for Gossip and Play. What content connected to the topic can help us enliven and enrich students' understanding by providing some gossip that they can engage in? What aspects of the content can be used for some form of game or fantasy play?

Aspects of the topic that might allow opportunities for gossip and play: The students can be given opportunities to take the parts of the three characters and, in small groups, invent some imaginary adventure they might have, each keeping to one character or another. Alternatively they could be in small groups, each group representing one of the characters—There, Their, or They're—and they could invent anecdotes about the other two, based on the characters developed for them.

3.2 Developing Embryonic Forms of Later Cognitive Tools. How can we encourage the use of some of the cognitive tools that come along with literacy?

Further cognitive tools that might give shape to the lesson or unit: Each of the characters could be imagined to have had great success as a pop star, or perhaps the three of them as a band. The students might be invited to draw how they imagine they would appear in their band style, based on their characters. Each of the characters might be interviewed—in groups of three, taking turns to interview each other—about their style of singing, which could further indicate something about their characters. Notes might be taken for a story to be written up for a pop music paper.

Students might be encouraged to find the homophone with the largest number of meanings, such as *right, rite, wright, write*—the Web sites indicated in the next subsection might help here. Or the one with the greatest divergence in the number of letters required in different words that sound the same. Or the ones with the fewest letters. Or the ones with nearly opposite meanings. The teacher might put up a "Homophones Records" sheet on the wall, and students could contribute whatever records they can discover.

4. Conclusion. *What is the best way to conclude the lesson or unit?*

4.1. Bringing the Story to a Satisfactory End. How does the story end? How do we resolve the conflict set up between the binary opposites? How much do we explain to the students about the binary oppositions and how explicit should we make them?

Concluding activity: You might let the students have some fun with inventing characters for such homophones as *beer* and *bier* or *foul* and *fowl* or *navel* and *naval* or *patience* and *patients*. For an excellent Web site devoted to homophones, giving hundreds of examples, see www.taupecat.com/personal/homophones/—and for an even more exhaustive collection, see www.marlodge.supanet.com/wordlist/homophon.html.

Or the students might be encouraged to make up their own jokes, starting with such examples as these (listed with acknowledgment to www.cooper.com/homophonezone/):

- Two vultures board an airplane, each carrying two dead raccoons. The stewardess looks at them and says, "I'm sorry, gentlemen, only one carrion allowed per passenger!"
- A mushroom walks into a bar, and the bartender says, "Get outta here—we don't serve your kind here." The mushroom responds, "Why not? I'm a fun-guy."

4.2. Suggesting the Mystery Behind the Topic. How do we give students some sense of the mystery attached to this topic?

Aspects of the topic that can give students a sense of mystery: Playing with homophones raises to consciousness features of language that we normally ignore or take for granted. How on earth does such a ramshackle business work so effectively? The teacher could give other examples of oddities: Why do we say "I run" and "he runs"? Why not "I run, you run, he run"? What is the extra "s" doing there? And if the same sounds can mean the same things, and sometimes the same word is used for different things, as with homonyms—the "pool" that one swims in as distinct from the "pool" that one plays on a table—then surely we have a very inefficient system of communication?

Why can't we rationalize it and make it more logical? And yet, despite the illogical features of language, somehow we manage to communicate effectively. And, even more strangely, the oddities are tied to language as an organic creation and we can see often how they help us communicate more clearly. (That extra "s" on "she runs," for example, works to reduce confusion; redundancy is common in language and means that even if we don't hear a part of the message, we can find clues to the meaning in other parts of a phrase or sentence. Computer languages need an inhuman precision to make sense of a message, whereas a natural language can handle a great deal of imprecision and yet convey meaning. The mystery of language can be exposed in a small way by such simple observations. Computers are generally hopeless at sorting out homophones.

The real mystery to hint at continually when teaching concerns the peculiarity of language as a unique form of behavior. It is a function of our bodies, yet such an odd one that it ties us together in unusual ways. Humans are "social animals" like no other. Many animals have some form of language, but none of them seems to have anything remotely like ours. No other creature recites elaborate invented stories. So a crucial step in education is always to expose what is mysterious about things that it is too easy to take for granted.

I don't expect teachers to give students lectures—as I have in the past three paragraphs. Rather the trick for the teacher is to simply mention these puzzles of language, to bring out the oddity of the way we shape air as it comes up through our necks and the astonishing range of things we can do with it.

5. Evaluation. *How can we know whether the topic has been understood, its importance grasped, and the content learned?*

Forms of evaluation: Any traditional forms of evaluation can be used to assess whether students understand the appropriate meaning of the different homophones studied this way. A common exercise would be to provide students with sentences in which they would have to choose between there/their/they're at the appropriate place. I suspect they would have little difficulty, having created stories with characters that indicate the proper spellings. An example of such a story is available at http://www.teachingideas.co.uk/english/homophonews.htm. (I owe this example, with thanks, to Moira Green, adult literacy organizer from the County Clare Reading and Writing Scheme, Ireland.)

Example Five: Heat

And one more example:

1. Locating Emotional Meaning. *What is emotionally engaging about the topic? How can it evoke wonder? Why should it matter to us?*

It can be difficult for a teacher to work up a personal emotional involvement with the topic of heat, and it has usually been taught for its informational content as a simplified science unit. The trick once again is to try to re-see the topic through the eyes of the students, to catch at what can stimulate the sense of wonder about it.

Sources of meaning: I find it is often useful, with science topics, to begin with the ancient Greek myths, because they usually present something central to the topic with great vividness, which I can then build the content around. (Those are, after all, the historical bases from which subsequent scientific understanding grew.) For heat, the myths offer a wide range of choices, with the myth of Prometheus being especially vivid.

Sources of emotional engagement: The vivid way in which the ancient myths make clear the power that control over heat gave human cultures and the terrible dangers inherent in that power.

2. Thinking About the Content in Story Form. *How can we shape the content so that it will have some emotional meaning? How can we* *best bring out that emotional meaning in a way that will engage the imagination?*

2.1. Finding Binary Opposites. What binary concepts best capture the wonder and emotion of the topic? If this were a story, what would the opposing forces be?
Main opposition: Heat as helper/heat as destroyer.
Possible alternative: Hot/cold.

2.2. Finding Images, Metaphors, and Drama. What parts of the topic most dramatically embody the binary concepts? What image best captures that content and its dramatic contrast?
Image or metaphor that captures the binary oppositions: Prometheus stealing fire from the gods and being punished by Zeus; Phaeton trying and failing to drive Apollo's fiery chariot across the sky; Hephaestus, whom the Romans called Vulcan, limping around his workshop.
Content that reflects binary oppositions: The way uses of heat in human cultures can benefit us or go out of control and destroy us.

3. Structuring the Body of the Lesson or Unit. *How do we teach the content in story form?*
Overall story structure of the lesson: So your initial teaching might begin with the myth stories that explain, in an emotionally engaging way, the vital importance of heat to human life—and its dangers. The daring of Prometheus in giving fire to humans, and the terrible punishment Zeus imposed on Prometheus, show the importance control of heat has played in human civilization. It is a power that has made us like the gods.
Phaeton's escapades show what destruction can follow when this terrible servant gets out of control: Phaeton is allowed to drive Apollo's fiery chariot—the sun—across the heavens. But he loses control and causes devastation on the earth. Even before the disaster, the god of light, Apollo, regretted granting to his child the fulfillment of such a wish and pleaded, "No, my child, choose something else. You ask for too dangerous of a gift. Even Zeus, the mighty god

of thunder, will not drive the chariot of the Sun. The horses breathe out flames and the chariot itself is fiery hot. So powerful are the steeds that I, a full-grown god, can barely restrain them. What chance would a mortal boy have? The journey is steep and at times I have grown dizzy looking down from the great heights at the Earth below. The path through the stars leads near great, dangerous creatures. You would have to pass Taurus, the giant bull, and gallop by the fierce lion. If you succeed in getting past them you would face the Scorpion with its huge deadly stinger and the pinching claws of the great Crab. I beg you to pick some other gift. Think of all the riches in the world or pearls from the boundless sea. Ask for any of these and I shall gladly give it to you."

Anyone unfamiliar with these stories can find them in any of a dozen tellings in books of Greek myths. It is very hard to make them dull.

The middle of the unit needs to elaborate the theme of heat as destroyer/heat as helper. It is not to be developed by simply putting relevant content into some logical sequence. Rather the teacher must think more as a storyteller developing a theme. So the content selected will be influenced by the theme. The best experiments, for example, are not so much those that get at key facts but those that expose key facts in light of the theme. It is what they expose about the constructive and destructive forces of heat that matters now. Such common experiments as using silver or matte black reflectors over glasses of water and measuring the temperatures of the water after they have stood in the sun for some time can be engaged with the theme through wondering how spaceships and astronauts can best be protected from the sun's heat in space. And so on. The difference in this approach is more a matter of context, of emotional quality, than of the typical content of such a unit. From here the teacher could move to discuss convection and conservation, in each case reflecting on heat's potential as destroyer and helper.

Or one might begin from the story of Hephaestus and lead into a study of volcanoes—which were assumed to be flames from Hephaestus' workshop. This could lead into ways to measure heat.

There are now a thousand lesson plans available on the Internet, any of which will suggest experiments teachers can perform to enhance students' understanding of heat. They can easily be incorporated into this unit, as long as each of them is presented as building on the theme of helper/destroyer. Usually they will work best if associated with one of the powerful stories with which the lesson began. In the process of moving from these initiating stories, students will learn that heat is a form of energy that moves from hot objects to cold ones, along with all the other usual information typically dealt with in such a unit, including debunking the common misconceptions about heat (sweaters are warm, and the like).

3.1. Locating Material That Can Provide Opportunities for Gossip and Play. *What content connected to the topic can help us enliven and enrich students' understanding by providing some gossip that they can engage in? What aspects of the content can be used for some form of game or fantasy play?*

Aspects of the topic that might allow opportunities for gossip and play: What's to gossip about heat? Well, it might be easy to ask students to talk about fires they have heard about or seen, perhaps one in their kitchen and how it was put out, or about the buildup of such heat that hard metals are reduced to flowing streams. It is easy to relate dramatic stories of fires to the deep lessons embedded in myths. Students will easily see that someone taking risks that go out of control seems like Phaeton. Some cases will be more like the carelessness and thoughtlessness of Daedalus's son, Icarus, who flew too close to the sun, melting the wax that held his wings together. (Don't try this at home!)

We know not to play with fire, but we can experiment with care to enlighten this wonderful servant that, if let out of control, can destroy us.

3.2. Embryonic Forms of Later Cognitive Tools. *How can we encourage the use of some of the cognitive tools that come along with literacy?*

Further cognitive tools that might give shape to the lesson or unit: Experiments with heating water and generating steam can tie in with the stories of Hero of Alexandria's steam engine (used for religious ceremonies!), and then that of James Watt. These stories need to catch the human purposes, hopes, fears, struggles of the individuals, and embed their discoveries and inventions in them as they relate to the theme. That is, you can provide opportunities for seeing features of experiments not just in terms of myths but also—providing a bridge to later cognitive tools—in terms of real characters and their achievements.

Students might be encouraged to discover records about heat. A sheet of "Heat Records" could be put up. What is the hottest recorded temperature on earth? What is the coldest? What was the most destructive volcanic eruption or explosion in recorded history? What is the most powerful engine humans have created? And so on.

4. Conclusion. *What is the best way to conclude the lesson or unit?*

4.1. Bringing the Story to a Satisfactory End. How does the story end? How do we resolve the conflict set up between the binary opposites? How much do we explain to the students about the binary oppositions and how explicit should we make them?

Concluding activity: Students might be asked to list the ways in which heat helps their lives, and the ways it is a danger to them or causes them some discomfort or pain. They might then be encouraged to weight the items they have on each side, and write or say whether they think our need for heat in our homes, schools, malls, and so on comes without some great cost. They might like to consider how far we might be behaving a little like Phaeton or whether we are always using Prometheus's gift wisely.

Another conclusion to this unit might come in considering the constructive and destructive potentials of heat in nuclear power—if the teacher thinks the particular class can handle such a topic. This urgent issue is still grasped in the terms given vivid form in the ancient Greek myth of Prometheus and Zeus. Nuclear energy promises a Promethean gift to human beings, but Zeus may wreak vengeance for our attempts to harness his godly power. The myth catches, that is, a way in which we still emotionally orient ourselves to the constructive and destructive potentials of heat.

4.2. Suggesting the Mystery Behind the Topic. How do we give students some sense of the mystery attached to this topic?

Aspects of the topic that can give students a sense of mystery: The story of Prometheus suggests a dimension of mystery about heat. It gives us a power that is at the heart of all human cultural life. Cooking their food changed the way our human ancestors could spend their time. Using fire to provide heat led to our ability to make better tools and weapons. (Depending on the age of the students, the teacher might try reading the Charles Mackay poem "Tubal Cain," about a man who spent his life "by the fierce red light of his furnace bright" forging weapons. But, sad at the destruction wrought with his weapons, he brooded long until he returned to his forge and made the first ploughshare. The poem has a strong rhythm and rhyme scheme, and might prove engaging even for quite young students.)

The sense of mystery is encouraged by the recognition of the vast power the control of heat has given to us. Virtually nothing the students can see around them was made without somewhere in the process or the making of the components the controlled use of heat. And what *is* heat? One can also give some indication of the idea of entropy as part of the enriching conclusion to this unit.

5. Evaluation. *How can we know whether the topic has been understood, its importance grasped, and the content learned?*

Forms of evaluation: Evaluation of such a unit might be gained from traditional kinds of evaluation instruments—from informal questions that assess students' knowledge of the basic facts and their understanding of their relationship to the main theme, or from more formal, "summative" assessments at the conclusion of the unit. What this kind of framework also calls for, however, might be something written, dramatized, or drawn that gives evidence of the emotional impact of the unit while using supporting knowledge, skills, and understanding. So students might be invited to express in some form those aspects of heat in their lives that they value most highly and those that they fear.

◆

I should stop with the examples. You can explore many others on the www.ierg.net Web site. And if you try a new one yourself, why not send it to the Web site to be added to those that are currently there?

I should mention also that the examples presented here are not supposed to be perfect illustrations of the framework in action. They are simply topics taken at random, which I have allowed the framework to shape. I hope the results suggest this exercise might be worth trying for yourself.

Chapter Two

A Tool Kit for Literacy

When students reach about seven or eight years their thinking tends to become what we commonly call more realistic. Their imaginary friends are no longer imagined and depart along the road Peter Pan resisted. Their rag dolls cease to speak to them, becoming silent and discarded, with other remnants of early years, in the cardboard box the new TV arrived in. And we don't any longer go through the Santa Claus routine, with the milk and cookies, which a parent gets to drink before going off to bed, leaving some decorous crumbs and perhaps a note of thanks from Santa.

That they give up belief in Santa, ghosts, imaginary friends, and whatever fantasies they were encouraged to take on board when younger is just one part of a complex shift in thinking that goes on. In this chapter I describe some features of that shift, focusing once again on the cognitive tools students usually have available for learning. In this case, they are a set of cognitive tools that come along with literacy. (By *literacy*, I suppose I need to add, I don't just mean acquiring crude coding and decoding skills, but taking on gradually the cultural resources that have developed with literacy.)

You can get a sense of the difference I am referring to by looking closely at the kinds of stories pre-literate children enjoy and those most enjoyed by literate children. In the earlier age period, the stories commonly have humanized animal characters—like Pooh Bear or Peter Rabbit—or fantastic characters with human characteristics—like Teletubbies. The events that occur in these stories are commonly not too bothered by realism—magic is an acceptable part of the story as long as the plot is carried forward, and no explanation is required for the impossible nature of the characters or their situation.

After literacy, the stories are commonly much more realistic, involving characters who do heroic but possible things—like *Anne of Green Gables* or *The Hardy Boys*. When fantasy elements are included, as in, say, *Superman* or *The Hulk* or other superheroes, there is a realistic, even if highly implausible, explanation provided—born on the planet Krypton, or caught up in some nuclear or genetic experiment that went wrong, and so on—and the superhero has to behave consistently within the newly explained boundaries of his (usually) fantasy context. *Star Trek*'s Mr. Data has to have an enigmatic genius who built him (or it). These differences between earlier magic and later heroism, which reflect a new sense of reality and its limits and how it works, are based on a set of cognitive tools that our modern forms of literacy bring with them.

Here are some of the main cognitive tools students will possess in greater or lesser degree as they master literacy:

The sense of reality is one of literacy's greatest potential gifts—and one of its great dangers. The development of disembedded, rational, logically structured forms of thinking is greatly eased by literacy. It has historically been the source of our understanding of the processes by which nature works and our increasing control over these processes, but it can come at the cost of our alienation from the natural world—so that we can see nature, for example, as a set of "resources" rather than as a complex system of which we are a part.

The extremes of experience and the limits of reality are among the features of reality that first and most powerfully engage students' imaginations as literacy becomes fluent. That is, the reality that we first engage imaginatively tends to be "romantic"; it most readily focuses on the extremes, on the most exotic and bizarre features of reality, on the most terrible and courageous events. This kind of material is familiar from sensational newspapers and TV shows, and from publications like *The Guinness Book of World Records*.

Association with heroes is the tool that enables us to overcome some of the threat of alienation involved in the new sense of reality. By associating with those things or people that have heroic qualities, we can gain confidence that we too can face and deal with the real world, taking on those qualities with which we associate. It gives us the ability to imbue any aspect of reality with heightened importance.

The sense of wonder is a key tool in our initial explorations of reality. It enables us to focus on any aspect of the world around us, or the world within us, and see its particular uniqueness. We can turn this sense of wonder on anything, recognizing the wonderful in every feature of the world. This tool can provide the gift that allows us to recognize something wonderful behind even the most routine and taken-for-granted things. The starting point of all science and all inquiries is "I wonder why. . . ."

Collections and hobbies

exemplify a tool of great power during these years. Students commonly put immense intellectual energy into collecting a set of something or engaging in a hobby. This urge to securely understand something can be used extensively in education.

Knowledge and human meaning

is the title I am giving to the tool that enables us to see beyond the surface of any knowledge to its source in human emotion. All knowledge is human knowledge, discovered or invented as a result of some human emotion, and seeing knowledge through the emotions that were involved with its past creation or current use helps us grasp its deeper human meaning.

Narrative understanding

is a tool related to our ability to best make sense of things when we can grasp their emotional impact. A narrative context for knowledge can establish its emotional importance while also conveying the knowledge—about physics or mathematics no less than about history or literature.

The capacities for revolt and idealism	are related tools during this period of life. Students both resist the adult world and shift to find a place within it, and they desire to see it as better than it is. Revolt implies an ideal, whose absence justifies the revolt.
Changing the context	is a tool that enables the imagination to grasp the richer meaning of any topic. The classroom is often an emotionally sterile place, so routine that one topic after a while begins to look like another. By shifting the context in which knowledge is learned—by use of often simple devices—students' imaginations can be brought vividly to life, engaging the material much more richly.
The literate eye	is a tool that develops as students become familiar with texts and such symbolic forms as the list, flowchart, and diagram. The shift to literacy reflects also a shift from dominance of the ear to the eye in gathering information. Certain activities can facilitate this shift and also show students how literacy can expand their powers to organize and use knowledge.
Embryonic tools of theoretic thinking	will be picked up while students mainly use the tools of literacy, and increasingly the new tools will be engaged as students become more

familiar with using abstractions and theoretic forms of thought. We need to provide opportunities for students to begin using some of the later tool kit even if in embryonic form. As with young children's use of embryonic tools of literacy, in Vygotsky's terms, this might be seen as drawing the students forward in their "zone of proximal development."

I recognize, again, that the kinds of subheadings employed here are not the usual fare of texts designed for teachers. But this oddity isn't due to simple ignorance about the daily tasks of teaching. These topics have been brought into focus by taking the engagement of students' imaginations as a central concern. If engaging students' imaginations is held steadily to the fore as a condition of successful teaching, then the kinds of categories I discuss represent the kinds of things to which we should attend.

If we think of our task as not just teaching knowledge and skills but also as introducing our students to the human source of the knowledge and skills they are learning, we will be able to make our teaching more engaging to their imaginations, more meaningful to them, and more interesting for ourselves, too.

The cognitive tools explored here are in most cases developments of tools introduced in Chapter One. I think of them as being "domesticated" by literacy. So the binary opposites become a fascination with extremes and limits, the mystery that doesn't worry much about reality in the earlier period becomes the sense of wonder focused on extremes and limits of reality, the stories become more complex narratives, and so on. Also the tools of Chapter One—stories, binary opposites, metaphors, mental images, and the rest—do not go away as students become literate. They are still available to be used in their original or more sophisticated forms.

Cognitive Tools

Let us look at each of these cognitive tools in a little more detail, focusing on how they relate to teaching.

The Sense of Reality

Imagine it is two and a half thousand years ago and you are a wealthy Greek visiting Egypt, being taken on a tour of some temples by an Egyptian priest. You have become a little irritated because you have already gathered that, while you think of yourself as educated and civilized, this priest clearly thinks of you as a barbarian up from Hicksville. You are, of course, familiar with the traditional stories of your people, about the great gods Zeus, Hera, and Apollo, and all the others who live on high Mount Olympus, and you are fascinated to learn ways in which those stories are like and unlike the traditional stories of the Egyptians. But one big difference becomes worryingly clear. You know that your myths tell of how the gods consorted intimately with human beings a couple of centuries earlier—in your great-grandparents' time, or a generation or two before. But today you are led into one of the inner rooms of a temple and the priest, with a smile—because he knows the stories of the Greeks—shows you a list of all the high priests who have served at the temple. Their names are etched in hieroglyphics on the wall with their dates in office. You gaze up, astonished, as the names and their dates go up and up, then onto another column, century after century into the past. What you see are records of human beings active in that temple, in much the same way as the priest beside you, through centuries in which your traditional stories claim only gods roamed the earth.

When it was first invented, alphabetic writing led to rational techniques of thinking that in turn led many educated Greeks to dismiss the myths they inherited from their parents' and grandparents' generations. They concluded that what one hoped or believed about the world was irrelevant to what was actually real. They claimed that a reality exists beyond any individual's or group's beliefs and that the proper task of the mind was to discover and display this reality. It led to a new kind of search for truth.

All very well, you might be wondering, but what has this to do with teaching today? Well, I think we can see surprising similarities between what happened in ancient Greece and what happens in children today as they learn to read and write. We can see the development of similar cognitive tools and a similar interest in reality. This similarity is a product of picking up and learning to use particular cognitive tools. One product of beginning to use literacy is a heightened sense of a separate reality, and—in most individuals—fascination with its limits and extremes.

The fairytale "Jack and the Beanstalk" typically engages four- and five-year-old children in Western societies. Children do not commonly interrupt the story to ask about the genetic makeup of bean seeds that can grow up to the sky, nor do they wonder what supports giants and their country up there. They accept magic as long as it keeps the narrative flowing and the story exciting. The story of *Anne of Green Gables*, which typically engages ten-year-old children in Western societies (and is, perhaps surprisingly, even more popular with children in some Asian countries), is not less a fiction than "Jack and the Beanstalk." Unlike Jack's story, however, it makes accommodations with reality that its young literate readers or hearers require, presenting them with a coherent and recognizable, though unfamiliar, world. Even fantasies like the Star Wars movies or the Harry Potter novels need explanations for why things are the way they are—accommodations to reality that mark them as a different genre of fiction from "Jack and the Beanstalk" or "Cinderella." Something happens to children in Western societies between five and ten years of age that makes the kind of stories they enjoyed when younger become unacceptable as they grow. The thing that happens is that children become literate in that peculiar alphabetic way started, as far as we can tell, by the Greeks.

That students are interested in reality might hardly come as earth-shattering insight to anyone. What is potentially interesting, though, comes from describing some of the ways reality engages the imaginations of students after they become fluently literate.

The Extremes of Experience and the Limits of Reality

The reason literacy encourages a new conception of reality and a fascination with its extreme and odd features is not hard to understand. If, with unusual generosity, I were to arrange to fly you to a north Italian hill town and invite you to explore it, you wouldn't pull out a magnifying glass and start examining the details of your hotel room's carpet and wallpaper, before working gradually down the corridor and into the street. You'd probably set about locating the main square and the cathedral, discovering where the town walls were, and examining the more unusual buildings. Your attention would also be drawn to the behaviors, clothing, artifacts, and customs most unfamiliar to you. That is, in any new environment we strive to orient ourselves by establishing the limits of the environment and its most outstanding features. It is a sensible strategy, and we see it vividly at work when literacy stimulates a new conception of reality. As Jerome Bruner puts it, "literacy comes into its full power as a goad to the redefinition of reality" (1988, p. 205). (For an exploration of why literacy should stimulate this new sense of reality, see Egan, 1997.)

Perhaps I should add a qualifier to this point about focusing on the limits of reality. In part, this common fascination we see in newly literate students with, say, the subject matter of *The Guinness Book of World Records* (Who was the biggest, or smallest, or hairiest person? Who had the longest fingernails? Who has pulled the heaviest weight with their teeth, and so on?) is a search for a kind of intellectual security about their own life and circumstances. They are not fascinated by who had the longest fingernails for that person's sake but because it tells them something about proper scale and about norms, by limiting the possible. That is, in a roundabout way they are seeking knowledge about themselves. So when I suggest that teaching will be more effective by occasionally engaging students with the limits of the real world and human experience, I don't mean that to suggest removing any focus on their everyday world. Their new knowledge should empower them to deal better with precisely that. The everyday world around them can become more meaningful, and meaningful in a new way, if they orient to it through attention to the limits or context within which it exists. So emphasis on the extremes and limits of reality does not remove students' attention from everyday experience; rather, it enables them to see it in a new light—a light that should give them greater security and confidence in dealing with it.

By looking at students' fascination with the content of such TV shows as *Ripley's Believe It Or Not* or with other sensationalist shows, comics, or papers, we can get a clue to what engages their imaginations. A part of the folklore of education—something I hear constantly repeated in teacher education programs and in books for pre-service teachers—is that one must always begin from what the student already knows. Indeed, the psychologist who described using "advance organizers" wrote that he considered this finding the most crucial contribution of psychology to education (Ausubel, 1968). It seems so obvious, especially after endless repetition. How can this principle explain why most students want to know who had the longest fingernails ever? Well, yes, students all have fingernails. But at this level the principle is trite. It suggests that you can interest students best by starting with what they are already familiar with in their environment. In my experience, at around the age of ten most students are bored out of their minds by the things in their local environment and are much more interested in the weird, strange, and exotic—in things most distant and different from their experience.

At around the age of ten most students are interested in the weird, strange, and exotic— in things most distant and different from their environment.

I sometimes offer this scenario to teachers as a joke example: Say you have to take your colleague Isabelle's class because she became ill suddenly. She left two lessons with appropriate materials ready, and it is a Friday afternoon, and you have been asked to keep the students engaged because they might have been disturbed by her sudden illness. The first lesson plan is "The structure of your local neighborhood," and the second is "The most daring spies in history." Which do you think might be more engaging to the students? Well, yes, I know one could, using all the principles explored here, make the local neighborhood exciting. But if the principle about starting with what the student already knows is supposed to engage the students' interest better, then the lesson on the neighborhood should win hands down. It doesn't. Quite the opposite—and that means something must be wrong with the principle. (For a more extensive description of what is wrong with it, see Egan, 2003.)

In the imaginative classroom we will commonly include whatever is extreme or strange or exotic about a topic. While examining the life cycle of some animal or insect, we will find it useful to compare it with those of the most astonishing creatures. Cicadas that live underground and emerge once every seventeen years, and breed in their trillions, then die, clogging towns and rivers and fields, capture one extreme of insect life cycles. When teaching about the Industrial Revolution we will illustrate the changes it brought about by searching out its most dramatic and astonishing achievements. So we might consider the sequence of building iron ships and bring into focus the achievements of Isambard Kingdom Brunel. After the early iron ships—weighing up to a few hundred tons—were built, he set about building his *Great Eastern*. That ship weighed in at about twenty-four thousand tons, required specially forged chains to launch, and nearly capsized—destroying the dock.

Association with Heroes

Remember what it was like when you were ten or eleven years old. You were at the mercy of bus schedules, teachers' requirements and school regulations, parents' commands, dress codes, and so on and on—in fact, while your own ego and sense of independence were beginning to develop, you seemed hemmed in by the endless laws, rules, and regulations of others.

One trouble with the sense of reality is that, initially at least, the student has little sense of just what the world's limits are or how the world works. This can be, and usually is, disturbing, perhaps a little frightening. Many of us forget the insecurity of discovering an autonomous reality beyond our knowing and control. But the mind has strategies for dealing with this potential source of insecurity. Perhaps the commonest strategy employed to meet this threat is to make a mental association with someone or something that seems able to overcome the threats posed by everyday reality—anything from a sports team or star to a political leader or a popular icon like Mother Teresa or Martin Luther King Jr., or a local institution such as a school or company. The power of forming such associations is so versatile that the range of objects seems limitless: the tenacity of a weed on a stormy rock face, the ingenuity that has created an insulated plastic cup, the beauty and power of an animal, the elegance of a mathematical proof.

The archetypical hero in the Western tradition has been a male, power-oriented doer of usually violent deeds. What characterizes the hero is an unusual degree of what I am calling great human qualities. Our stock of heroes provides a wide range of qualities with which we can associate. The hero can embody unusual degrees of such qualities as sanctity, compassion, selflessness, elegance, wit, ingenuity, patience, or whatever, equally as well as testosteronic violence. So we can see a saint, a nurse, a scientist as heroic, no less than the debased successors of Ulysses and Sir Galahad whom we find, muscle-bound, battling in video arcades.

A point to emphasize about this early literate ability to associate with great human qualities: students tend to focus on heroes, as I have here. But it is not the hero, the particular pop star or football player, or the idea or institution or whatever, that is the object of the association. Rather, it is the human quality that the hero embodies. At one level this may seen obvious, but it is important to make the distinction to be able to use this characteristic flexibly when teaching.

That is, there's no need to be constantly dragging heroic figures into the classroom to draw on the instructional value of this cognitive tool. Instead, be alert to the fact that great human qualities can be found in anything, as I argued earlier; in the tenacity of that weed on a rock face, the persistence of stones, the serenity of cats, the productive industry of worms, the rage of storms. Anything, as I've said, can be seen in human terms—such terms will not give a complete view of any topic, but they will give one engaging view, and onto that you can add others. And most imaginatively engaging among human qualities are those that promise us an enlargement of our powers.

Another feature of human qualities is that they are inevitably emotional in some degree. We are not indifferent about our heroes; they engage our emotions. Football players or pop stars often attract degrees of emotion that astonish those who do not share an association with them.

Teaching rarely seems like a particularly emotional activity. Some see it as a job to be performed with as much professional efficiency as possible, and, while they recognize occasions that are "emotional," perhaps due to a clash of personalities or to some event that occurs in class that moves everyone, they tend not to think of the instructional activities as properly or routinely involving emotions, especially if teaching math or science, say. Most teachers probably do not plan their teaching in a way that involves reflection on the emotions to be evoked in class. Yet an implication of this cognitive tool is that we should do precisely that.

Perhaps it would be wise to add that evoking emotional responses to the materials of instruction does not require a classroom to be a site of tears or elation all day long. Emotions come in many forms and endless degrees. Human beings are, after all, in David Kresch's celebrated term, "perfinkers"; we "perceive/feel/think" together. Attention to heroic human qualities in teaching will underline the importance of perceiving, feeling, and thinking of students as individuals who are not simply thinkers when learning but are people whose senses and emotions must also be engaged if the teaching is to be most effective.

What is going on when people make these kinds of associations with sports heroes, film stars, tenacious weeds, or elegant proofs? It is at least in part a response to the threats posed by reality. Students (and adults) form associations with those who seem best equipped to overcome the threats that hem them in. The hero is like us, or like what we would wish to be, hemmed in by the world but somehow overcoming it in a way we would want to emulate. The sports or movie star has the strength, power, freedom, money that the student lacks but desires.

Like other cognitive tools that come along with literacy, this capacity does not simply go away as students' minds become more sophisticated. If you pause to consider who are your heroes, or what institutions or ideals or objects you form such associations with, you may discover what you still feel insecure about.

In the imaginative classroom we can use the cognitive tool of associating with heroic qualities to highlight almost any feature of the curriculum. It becomes a way to make things significant and to engage students' growing capacity to form such associations. For example, one can focus on any object—say, a book on the desk—and project into it some heroic qualities. In the case of the book, one might highlight the millennia of human ingenuity that have created this compact object crammed with tiny symbols that serve as an externalized memory, able to hold an endless array of information and convey the emotions and experience of other people in distant times and places. Human ingenuity has made the crammed pages hospitable to the eye by means of tiny punctuation marks and divisions within the text. These tiny marks helped to democratize reading, and have probably had more influence on human affairs than all the armies of history. Well, you can see how one can romanticize the object: highlight it, mark it off from its surroundings, making it an object with which students can form an association—associating themselves with that human ingenuity. Asking students to look at the book you lift from the desk in such terms is the kind of thing that need take no more than a couple of minutes, but can greatly enrich their sense of what books are.

This ability to project into objects the qualities that then enable students to associate with them easily—if you follow that doubling-back-on-itself procedure—is an important cognitive tool in making any topic lively and engaging. You can "heroize" almost any element of the curriculum. Those earthworms your class is to study become heroic farmers, tilling the soil through vast labors; the punctuation marks are the heroes that democratized reading, making the page hospitable to the eye and easy for all to manage; details of the anatomy of the eel can be seen through the heroic ingenuity and persistence of the people who discovered them.

The Sense of Wonder

Related to our ability to make associations with heroic qualities is our ability to see any object as wonderful. It is easiest to feel the emotion of wonder in the face of the more dramatic features of the natural world—the mountain view, the gold and scarlet sunset, the vast waterfall, the immensity of space. But the overflow of powerful feelings that accompanies wonder can, like heroic associations, be directed to almost any object. Wonder is the attitude of mind captured by the poet Yeats: "everything we look upon is blest."

And, yes, it isn't very realistic to expect teachers to maintain such an energetic mental state while collecting the students' papers or writing up next week's assignment, and, no, we can't go through life in such a state all the time. But, yes, it is possible to plan teaching such that we will bring this state of wonder to bear on topics with some frequency.

Wonder can be an engine of intellectual inquiry. It is a part of literate rationality's persistent questioning, a more directed kind of questioning than is common earlier in the young child's incessant "why?" Wonder can be silent in front of nature's grandeur, but it mostly encourages us to ask questions. "I wonder . . ." is the start of scientific thinking. I wonder why the bathwater rises as I sink into it? I wonder how many worms there are in the garden? I wonder why the sky is blue? The world becomes an object of wonder and inquiry.

Stimulating wonder energizes the literate mind. People can, of course, learn to be literate in a way that is crudely utilitarian, and the utilitarianly literate person may simply think "literally"—that is, not using literacy's power to evoke wonder.

Stimulating wonder energizes the literate mind.

In the imaginative classroom, then, we will be sensible to attend to ways to evoke a sense of wonder related to the topics at hand. This will require the teacher to reflect on each topic and locate what is wonderful within it. Anything—yes, anything—seen in the right light, can be seen to be wonderful. Even if the lesson involves dealing with the everyday transactions of shopping, the teacher can draw attention to the astonishing variety of goods brought from all the corners of the world, the ingenuity that has gone into arranging food in hygienic containers with stunning efficiency, the work of generations of chemists and physicists that has gone to making such taken-for-granted products as toothpaste, fruit juices, frozen peas, and so on. This does not demand lengthy factual lessons on the background of each item, but rather a constant alertness to the wonder of the shop. It is hard for some people to pull back from utilitarian routines, but the teaching task required to stimulate imagination involves the teacher in constantly locating the immediate objects of the lesson in the wider context of wonder. A part of imaginative teaching is to locate something wonderful in every lesson; doing so will not only make learning easier for the student, it will also make the lesson more interesting and satisfying for the teacher. I can't emphasize this enough.

This sense of wonder underlying the daily routine stuff of life is hardly a novel observation. A. N. Whitehead, in his essay "The Rhythm of Education" (1967, first published in 1922), discusses the importance of evoking a sense of "romance" when first introducing a topic to students. He talks about "the vividness of novelty . . . the excitement consequent on the transition from the bare facts to the first realization of the import of their unexplored relationships" (pp. 17–18).

Mention of excitement and vividness can, perhaps, deter the average teacher, who knows indeed that teaching can and should involve these qualities in some degree, but the deterrence comes from the seeming claim that classes should invariably be neuron-poppingly exciting all day long. I don't think Whitehead means that, and nor do I, though I recognize that too-frequent mention of *wonder* and so on can give an impression of not being aware of the realities of the everyday activities of teaching. Some of the trouble—between words and interpretation—perhaps comes from words like *romance* and *wonder* being taken on one hand as too exotic and on the other as too literal. That is, Whitehead is not expecting students and teachers to be constantly transported by romance in some B-movie sense. Rather, his idea suggests that the teacher should try to keep fresh and vivid for the student the genuinely wonderful human achievements that are a part of all topics in the curriculum. How one may aim to do that day by day is the task of the following chapters. But from this discussion of wonder and Whitehead's related *romance* comes a principle that can help us inject these qualities into our planning and teaching.

Collections and Hobbies

It has always struck me as odd that I hardly ever see in educational texts much concern about students' hobbies and collections. The activities involved in these related and sometimes overlapping self-chosen tasks clearly engage students' intellectual energy like hardly anything else. What is going on? Why are they doing it? And why don't educators focus more attention on these activities and learn from them?

Well, what is going on and what's to learn? One part of the drive to collect and engage in some hobby seems clearly connected to the insecurity mentioned already about the growing recognition of an indeterminately large reality. Students can develop one kind of security by associating with those qualities that seem best able to overcome its apparent threats. Another kind of security can come from learning that reality is not infinitely large. A common route to the latter kind of security is to get an exhaustive understanding of some part of reality. By collecting "the whole set," as commercial interests suggest you do as they exploit this urge, you recognize that the world is manageable, limited, understandable.

Even if you never collect the whole set—of comics or stamps or dolls or action figures—you gain a curious satisfaction in learning what constitutes the whole set. The security of knowing all there is to know about however small an area of knowledge is immensely satisfying. Even though a student will not collect all the songs of Ani DiFranco (because there are always unreleased and bootlegged tapes somewhere) or own all the Victorian postage stamps produced in Canada, there is great satisfaction in the search and in collecting as many parts of the set as possible.

The drive to collect and to develop a hobby seems to begin typically with literacy, reaching a peak in puberty, dying out or losing a lot of its energy with the development of theoretic thinking.

No doubt there are other psychological mechanisms in play in collecting and hobbies, but the one identified here has some clear educational implications. Once the imagination is caught up with some area of knowledge in a way that provides the student with the chance to "collect the set" or know exhaustively about it and "become an expert," then great energy can be released in learning. The trick is in isolating aspects of a topic that are exhaustible in a manner that can allow the student to learn nearly everything about it.

Teachers might be reasonably skeptical that the enthusiasm that students bring to collecting songs by their favorite pop stars or learning about motorcycles cannot be so easily harnessed to learning about algebra or science. As an experiment, teachers might try asking their students what they collect or what hobbies they pursue. I ask the students in my education courses this question regularly, and they are usually astonished by the range of things collected or the kind of hobbies others have. Often, by their comments, they indicate they have no understanding of why other students would collect some of the range of things they do, or why some have the hobbies they developed. That is, as with the human qualities with which we can form associations, so the things that engage the collecting instinct or engage students in a hobby seem almost random. Almost anything will work if the right triggers are available. For the teacher the trick is to recognize what these triggers are, and then make them available in teaching algebra or whatever.

One crucial trigger is to "collect the set"; provide some area within a topic that the students can learn exhaustively. This is different from allotting chunks of a topic for students in groups to do a project on. They may well be encouraged to work in groups, but the trick is for the teacher to locate something exhaustible within the topic.

In the imaginative classroom teachers will be alert to the powerful urge students have to find intellectual security amid all the "stuff" that is out there to be learned. As with learning the extremes of reality, the teacher can provide large posters, maybe mounted on a wall, onto which students might enter "records" they have discovered about a topic. If the topic is the study of eels, students can "collect" the longest eels, the shortest eels, the fattest eels, the slimmest eels, the ugliest eels, the most beautiful eels, the longest-living eels, the shortest-living eels, the strangest eels, the most voracious eels, the most dangerous eels, the eels with the longest migrations, and so on. Or they might be given the task of charting the changes eel larvae go through. If students are engaged in making exhaustive lists, preferably of extreme features, or charting exhaustive knowledge of something dramatic, such activities will commonly trigger the cognitive tool evident in collecting and hobbies.

And how do teachers get students to make a hobby of algebra or what could teachers have students collect in algebra?

The teacher can give one group of students a very small number, such as the measurement of the thickness of a typical cell membrane, which comes in around 0.00000001 meter thick. They will recognize that this is slightly awkward to deal with. Another group can be given a very large number, say, the number of molecules in a cubic centimeter of oxygen at standard temperature and pressure, which comes in at roughly 602,000,000,000,000,000,000,000 (give or take a few trillion). The groups can be invited first to discover more very small and very large numbers, and, once astonished by the amount of a page they can use up writing them down, they can be invited to explore on the Internet ways of using algebra to make such numbers manageable. (There are a number of excellent sites that will explain scientific notation clearly—for example, see http://library.thinkquest.org/20991/alg/sci_not.html.)

Knowledge and Human Meaning

Imagine standing at night among the stacks of a large library. Imagine also that you are the only person in the building. It would be easy to feel as though the odd noises you hear are whispers from the books, and that, as the night goes on, the whispers will get louder and louder, becoming deafening. Wandering past row after row of books, you may feel a bit daunted, or frightened even, by all the knowledge that people have accumulated. In fact, for anyone in the knowledge business, such an experience can be a bit depressing, making brutally clear how minuscule an amount of knowledge any one of us can accumulate. But it is useful to recognize that the only knowledge in that vast library is what is in your head. What is in the books is merely desiccated code, not voices. Knowledge is not symbols—symbols are just reminders of knowledge: hints, pointers. Knowledge is a function of the living tissue of our living brains.

Obvious as this point is, I think we often forget it. We can easily forget that learning the symbols in which knowledge is encoded is no guarantee at all of knowing. All knowledge is human knowledge; it is a product of human hopes and fears and passions. The primary trick in bringing knowledge to life from the codes in which we store it is through the emotions that gave it life in the first place in some other mind. Knowledge, again, is part of living human tissue;

books and libraries contain only desiccated codes. The business of education is enabling new minds to bring old knowledge to new life and meaning.

Knowledge is part of living human tissue; books and libraries contain only desiccated codes.

Scientific knowledge, especially as stacked in textbooks, has an aura of objectivity; it is secure, uninfluenced by what readers might hope or fear, a solid assertion of what is true. Or, at least, that is what we are supposed to think. That kind of security and objectivity has commonly been seen as one of the great products of the development of literacy. But literacy had been employed for a great variety of tasks before it was used in the development of science. We might do well to focus on the kind of knowledge that was found engaging and meaningful by people during the early years of literacy's use. The educational trick is to show knowledge as the product of human beings' ingenuity, energy, passions, hopes, fears, and so on. People like us made it, invented it, discovered it, formulated it for human purposes, with human motives.

Instead of representing knowledge to the newly literate as a given—telling them the rules for comma use or mathematical operations and making them do exercises till they get the rules right— you can make the knowledge memorable and meaningful by re-embedding it in the contexts of its original invention or human uses. When students learn a mathematical algorithm, for example, by seeing who invented it and for what purpose or how it is used for some dramatic purpose today, they absorb it more easily, understand it better, and remember it.

In the imaginative classroom, we will bear in mind that everything we teach has a human source—the comma was invented by someone and has had astonishing effects in human history, the life cycle of the eel was discovered by someone and fascinates those who learn about it, geometric theorems were invented by someone and used by people to achieve amazing things—and that bringing to the fore the human emotions, ambitions, intentions, fears, and so on, we can expect to engage our students' imaginations in learning. The imaginative classroom will be full of people, past and present, and full of their voices, hopes, fears, and passions. By using this cognitive tool in our teaching, we will in turn help students develop it further, enabling them to see human emotions behind and below the surface features they have to deal with. Such a tool simply enriches life.

In teaching the geometric theorem for calculating height, the teacher might begin by telling the story of the ancient Greek Thales as a tourist in Egypt, fascinated by the pyramids:

> One day the guide told his small group that the pyramid they had ridden out to that morning was the tallest of all the pyramids. Thales asked, "How tall is it?"
>
> "Uh . . . well, I don't know," said the guide, embarrassed. "I guess if we climbed to the top and let down a rope. . . . Hmmm, that wouldn't be any good, it would only measure the side."
>
> The other tourists wondered how anyone could measure the height of a pyramid, while Thales just seemed to be walking around.
>
> "OK. Your pyramid is 329 cubits high," Thales said.
>
> Everybody was astonished. How could Thales have worked it out?

The teacher could introduce this story after some preliminary work had been done on triangulation, and lead into showing that if Thales knew how tall he was, and how long his shadow was, and was able to pace off the length of the pyramid's shadow, he could figure out the height of the pyramid. The students are learning the same geometric theorem as those who do not have it tied, even in this simple way, in some human source. But the students who spend some thought on working out what Thales was doing pacing round in the desert sands, and who feel the ingenuity of his clever solution, are likely to learn it better and remember it longer—and find it more meaningful and engaging.

Narrative Understanding

In Chapter One I suggested that the story was crucial in early learning because it was the tool that enables us to bring curriculum content and emotion together to make knowledge more fully meaningful to the student. That remains largely true for older students, but the kind of story that engages them is different from the basic story structures more common in early years. Instead of continuing to use the term *story*, and to avoid possible confusion, I will switch to the word *narrative* for equivalent techniques tailored to this level of understanding (perhaps creating a whole new kind of confusion).

A narrative is a continuous account of a series of events or facts that shapes them into an emotionally satisfactory whole. It has in common with a story that shaping of emotion, and so the words are often used synonymously, but it is different in that narratives can be less precisely tied into a tight story, less concerned with emotion, more varied, more open, more complex. That is, I want to use *narrative* to indicate the greater variety and openness of the stories that prove most useful as students become fluently literate, though I do want to preserve the importance of shaping events and facts to affect emotions.

To echo Chapter One, instead of thinking of our lessons and units as sets of objectives we hope to attain, we can think of them as good narratives with which we hope to engage students' imaginations and emotions.

Brian Sutton-Smith wrote, "The mind is . . . a narrative concern" (1988, p. 22). This is a view that is becoming increasingly widely accepted. Jerome Bruner has also elaborated a view of the mind as involving a crucial narrative dimension (1986). The older view of the mind as an elaborate calculating organ with reason as its mode of calculating has become increasingly untenable. Rationality is not simply a set of computing skills; the mind works as a whole, and its whole includes our bodies and our emotions and imaginations. We have discovered—or at least people who didn't know these things all along have discovered—that we make sense of our experience and the world in narratives, that we can recall items in narratives better than in logically ordered lists, that we organize our memories more profoundly and reliably according to emotional rather than logical associations, and so on.

Rationality is not simply a set of computing skills;
the mind works as a whole, and its whole includes
our bodies and our emotions and imaginations.

Any fact or event, according to Alasdair MacIntyre, "becomes intelligible by finding its place in a narrative" (1981, p. 196). And yet, developing the tool of narrative has tended to receive less attention than developing logical skills, which are seen to be more productive. But they are not separate chunks of our minds; logical skills need the development of narrative tools to be used most effectively.

Learning to follow a narrative is a vital intellectual accomplishment. Efficiently following a narrative means being able to allot significance, recognize what is important, fit parts together from textual clues, construct emotional meaning while registering events and facts, recognizing sequences through emotions despite logical gaps in a narrative, and a range of other intellectual skills. As Northrop Frye put a related point: "The art of listening to stories is a basic training for the imagination" (1963, p. 49). Being able to follow a narrative is crucial for efficient learning and understanding of almost any topic in the curriculum. It also enhances our manipulation of possibilities—which is what enables students to apply something learned in one context to another.

One obvious reason why it would be desirable to pay more attention to narrative in education is that it is accessible to everyone. The focus on what Margaret Donaldson has called "disembedded" logical skills has disproportionately favored the minority of children who develop such skills early (1978). While those logical skills are important, when developed at the expense of narrative tools the results tend to be people who are good at doing specific things, but who lack flexibility and imagination. As Robert Coles notes, "A respect for narrative [is] everyone's rock-bottom capacity, but also a universal gift, to be shared with others" (1989, p. 30). That is, if our aim is the education of all children, then it makes sense to attend to this basic and important intellectual skill we share and can use relatively easily for learning.

In the imaginative classroom we will be alert to narrative possibilities for all topics. Sometimes a brief narrative of a person's life can provide a context that makes particular knowledge meaningful and imaginatively engaging. To teach Pythagoras's theorem without some mention of Pythagoras's strange life and astounding and prophetic ambitions would be to ignore exactly what can make the theorem more generally meaningful and engaging. To teach the life cycle of the eel without mentioning the amazing work of Johannes Schmidt in discovering that life cycle would be to greatly impoverish the topic. To study trees without exploring their central role in human history would be to miss out on what can make the botanical information gripping.

Revolt and Idealism

Students are exploring the roles they will take in the adult world and simultaneously resisting those roles. The early years tend to be powerless; students are told what to wear, how to behave, what to believe, and so on. As they grow through puberty, the constraints that hem them in remain despite the increasing independence they feel, even if initially only in small ways.

The revolt or resentments that students commonly feel are also fueled by their sense of an ideal world or circumstances. It is the denial of their ideal that leads to the revolt against those who deny them. But this is also the time at which students begin to form not only simple ideals about the kind of freedom that would allow them to color and shave their hair as they wish but also about the world at large. They would like the world to be peaceful, they would like people to stop polluting the environment, and so on. The adult world's continuing war and pollution stimulate more general and diffuse revolts.

In this dynamic we can see an important cognitive tool: the ability to imagine a world or particular circumstances that are superior in some way to the reality the students experience, to recognize those features of the adult world that prevent their ideal's being realized, and to revolt against them. And how can we use this cognitive tool in everyday teaching? Well, in nearly every topic we teach, math no less than history, there will be examples of conventions or obstructions that prevent the achievement of some ideal, and there will also be someone or some idea prevailing against the conventions or obstructions.

In the imaginative classroom, when presenting Boyle's Law, say, this principle will invite us to expose students not simply to the law itself but to Robert Boyle's struggle against conventional ideas, and particularly against the prevailing belief (argued by Descartes and Hobbes among others) that a vacuum could not exist. The great authorities claimed that ether pervaded space. Boyle's experiments couldn't locate this ether, so he dismissed it—and it has stayed dismissed! The students might also be reminded that since Aristotle's time, and before, it was believed that everything was made up from the four elements of earth, air, fire, and water. Instead, Boyle argued that matter was made up from different combinations of tiny primary particles, which is how we still conceive of matter. Just a small amount of background on this extraordinary Irishman, and a sense of his struggles against fixed beliefs and orthodoxies, can engage students' imaginations in his discoveries that transformed chemistry and changed our understanding of our world in important ways.

Teaching the arts in general, of course, provides an embarrassment of riches in seeing works of literature or other arts as having struggled, in the lives of their creators, against the barriers of convention and opposition of one kind or another. And much the same is dramatically true of the sciences as well. It is no great strain to provide some small background information to show what the artist or scientist was up against. Like all these tools, however, it won't be equally useful in all cases, and in some won't be of any use at all. But the imaginative teacher will be alert to the struggles people have undergone to bring into reality their ideals, usually in the face of opposition, abuse, and derision.

Changing the Context

One of the enemies of effective teaching and learning is students' (and teachers') boredom, and one of the triggers of boredom is excessive familiarity and taking things for granted. John Bennett's "law of mental declension" suggests that we always deal with any problem with the least outlay of intellectual energy possible (1967). Think of learning to drive a car. Initially you have to give it all your attention because the problems of keeping this moving mass of metal on the road are significant. After a while, as developing skill enables you to coordinate all the required movements of hands, eyes, and feet, you still give a lot of intellectual energy to the task of driving because it is a challenge you are beginning to master. After some years of driving, you hardly notice the acts you perform to get the car from A to B; it becomes quite automatic.

Bennett suggests that this "mental declension" applies to all features of our lives. What is needed to stimulate the mind to move up the scale of intellectual energy it gives to any task is the introduction of a challenge.

What has all this to do with teaching? Well, one problem with the classroom is its largely unvarying context, which students gradually come to take for granted. Remembering Marshall McLuhan's slightly mischievous claim that "the medium is the message," we can see how the unvarying nature of the classroom can make much of what students experience in classrooms take on a uniform and somewhat boring cloak (1964). At least, this is what most of the large-scale surveys of students' experience of school tell us.

One way we can plan a challenge to the imagination-suppressing taken-for-grantedness of the daily classroom is to change the context

now and then. This doesn't mean redecorating so much as changing the kind of attention required of the students.

When I was doing my teacher training, just after the Civil War,
an ancient teacher (maybe forty-five or fifty) told me that if I wanted
the students to learn and remember some important fact then I
should walk into the classroom with a huge pile of books balanced
precariously. Slowly, with the pile threatening to tip to one side or
another, I should move to the center of the room, pause for a few
seconds, then drop the books in a heap. "You've got about ten seconds in which you can teach anything," he said. I tried it on the
chemical formula for salt. When the books fell, and the students all
looked at me in the silence, I slowly said, "NaCl." Over the next
few months, and in a few cases years later, when I asked any of the
students from this class, every one of them remembered the chemical formula for salt, even though they couldn't remember many
other formulae we covered in that unit.

I am not recommending that you wreck your library just to
teach a few facts. Rather, this is a way of demonstrating that the peculiar situation challenges the students and greatly increases their
attention and readiness to learn. So what to look for are ways of
more routinely (and less destructively!) changing the context in a
way that presents an appropriate challenge to students.

In the imaginative classroom one common way to do this is for
the teacher to take on the role of a character involved in what is
being taught. When teaching science, come in one day as Marie
Curie and present her work on radioactivity as though from her perspective. Describe her early work, the opposition she faced, expressing her emotional response and what motivated her, and the
array of honors she received, including the two Nobel prizes. An
old-fashioned hat and a vaguely Polish accent is all that will be
needed to significantly shift the context. (Male teachers might have
more success with Einstein, though some might look quite charm-
ing in the Marie Curie hat!)

In a history class one can change the context by asking the students to pretend to be participants in the events being studied, and
perhaps to debate the conflicting positions of the combatants. In

math a few old sheets can transform the class into a bunch of ancient Greeks discovering some geometrical theorem. A group of teachers might get together and plan a semester around one topic—say, edible grains. The whole curriculum can then be planned for the semester—around the history of edible grains and their role in human settlements, the geography of the sources of the grains, where they were planted and why, the mathematics of grain production, sales, and distribution, the biology of grains and their growth, and so on. The students can each be given roles in such a semester-long unit, such that their whole school day would be involved with their tasks in the growth, development, distribution, and study of grains.

Who knows, you might discover a hidden actor inside, delighted at this kind of break in routine. The effects on learning can be surprisingly dramatic.

There are endless ways to shift the context so that the routine classroom becomes a place where students never quite know what to expect. It is no longer the usual place where the usual activities can be relied on and taken for granted. The imagination can transform the classroom, without anything much in the way of decorations or props—though those can sometimes help.

> *Shift the context so that the classroom becomes a place where students never quite know what to expect.*

One of the tools students have available is this ability to heighten awareness and attention in response to a simple challenge or puzzle. Traditional ways of changing contexts have involved such activities as field trips. But I focus on a somewhat different kind of context changing, a kind that is concerned more with the intellectual activity required of the student and that doesn't take hugely elaborate preparation by the teacher—though of course there's no end to the time and energy the teacher can expend, as all teachers know.

The Literate Eye

During this period, when literacy comes increasingly to influence students' thinking, the eye is becoming crucial in accessing information. This has many consequences, which are subject to some dispute among scholars interested in the effects of literacy. But, whatever the outcome of those arguments, it is clear that literacy leads to some techniques for organizing information that are both important and engaging for students to learn. I have mentioned earlier the value of making and manipulating lists, flowcharts, and diagrams. In many subject areas, such techniques can enlarge students' engagement in gaining control over areas of complex knowledge. Use of such tools also exercises and develops them in students.

Today many of these tools are built into computer programs, and certainly learning to use databases and other programs that aid organization and retrieval of knowledge can enhance this cognitive tool in students.

Embryonic Tools of Theoretic Thinking

While the cognitive tools of literacy are becoming increasingly sophisticated, students are also beginning to use some of the tools that I describe in Chapter Three: the sense of abstract reality, the sense of agency, the grasp of general ideas and their anomalies, the search for authority and truth, and meta-narrative understanding. In the imaginative classroom, especially with students who are making good progress developing the cognitive tools of literacy, teachers might want to bear in mind the burgeoning interest in general schemes, theories, ideologies, metaphysical ideas, and the other inhabitants of the theoretical world. The final example in Chapter Two and a Half suggests a quite easy way to build an embryonic theoretical dimension into any topic, using the study of trees as an illustration. The trick is often just to be aware of the main arguments that take place about the topic one is dealing with. If it is eels, then some attention might be given to the threats to their habitats, raising, even if only briefly, issues of environmental challenge against the desires of development. This will no longer be presented in terms of a simple binary conflict, but rather as competing interests in which we are complicit. It is not enough now to regret habitat destruction, students must recognize that things they want, like iPods or computers, are made at an environmental price. That is, for the theoretic students' growing sense of agency, these conflicts are to be located within each person, not simply conflicts "out there," allowing the student to easily associate with the "good guys."

◆

By focusing attention on students' imaginations, we bring to the fore a set of somewhat unfamiliar topics. Or at least, if they are familiar enough in our everyday experience—heroes, the extreme and exotic, and so on—they are not so familiar in texts on teaching. My aim is to make these cognitive tools central to the task of helping students successfully attain flexible understanding.

Using this approach, teachers can think of instruction not only in terms of acquisition of skills and knowledge but also as an enlargement of students' cognitive tool kits. In fact, my hope is that it will become clear that focusing first on the cognitive tools will make it much easier to teach the skills and knowledge. The teacher will be both using the cognitive tools students have available and, reciprocally, developing those tools by exercising and enlarging students' use of them.

That is, to emphasize a point, knowledge and skills and cognitive tools are not competitors. Students can't develop cognitive tools without learning knowledge and skills, and while the point can be pushed too far, it is generally true that the more knowledge and skills students learn the more highly developed their cognitive tools become. So this brings to the fore the crucial role that expanding knowledge plays in driving the development of literate cognitive tools. Understanding becomes rich and flexible and strong as it is supported and challenged by the constant growth of knowledge. A central feature of imaginative education is that the student needs to know a lot if the imagination is to develop adequately and to work effectively. Ignorance is not a condition that favors the development of imagination.

> *Ignorance is not a condition that favors the*
> *development of the imagination.*

In concluding, it might be worth reflecting on the set of cognitive tools of literacy and on how they help us to see why Anne of Green Gables and Harry Potter, Luke Skywalker and Officer Ripley, Cleopatra and Alexander engage people's imaginations, and how we might use those tools in everyday teaching.

Chapter Two and a Half

Examples in Everyday Classrooms

Knowledge is preserved in dead codes—desiccated symbols in books—and the teacher's daily job is to raise the dead, to bring the codes back to life in new minds. The cognitive tools of literacy mostly focus on humanizing knowledge to make it accessible, placing it in realistic environments—even if it is the dramatic, exotic, or extreme features of the real world that appeal to students' imaginations.

To do this vital job, it helps to think of the classroom as more than a place in which students are prepared for the skills and tasks that adult life holds for them. Of course, this must be a part of what happens in the classroom. But especially during the years from around seven or so to around fifteen or sixteen, the cognitive tool I've called "changing the context" suggests a general shift in how we might think of the classroom. Our teaching job might be made a bit easier if we were to see the classroom as sharing something of the character of Dr. Who's "Tardis." Dr. Who was the hero of what began as a British science fiction TV show aimed at, and immensely popular with, the oral and newly literate age groups. The Tardis, from the outside, looked like a police call box or kiosk of the kind that used to be common in Britain before they were made redundant by the cell phone. But inside, it was a space/time ship. Dr. Who could travel anywhere in the universe and through time, popping up where and when the plot required, except when things— to add to the drama—went wrong, of course.

Some purposes for classroom activities emphasize blending the school with the outside environment, but engaging the imagination with reality, paradoxically, can be helped by emphasizing the separateness of the classroom from the everyday world outside the school. The classroom can be perceived as a staging point from which students can move readily to many environments in time and space, of which that of daily life outside the school is only one. We might imagine entering a classroom as a little like entering Dr. Who's time/space kiosk. Once aboard and under way, we might take off to any time or place.

Clearly such imagining does not transform the usual desks and windows and floor covering, but adopting this conception of the classroom can transform our sense of what is appropriate and possible in it. Teacher and students might have fun organizing lessons that take the idea halfway literally. The teacher might begin lessons by inviting the students to pull over them an imaginary protective sheet, and then to close their eyes. The techniques of guided imagery can be used to stimulate images appropriate to the topic of the next lesson: "You are slowly rising into the air. . . . You are safe. . . . Let us slip into the stream of time. You can feel its soft wind in your hair and on your face. The wind of time is warm and sweet. See below you . . ." and so on. Two or three minutes can suffice to set students into a medieval mathematics class in Pisa, or into an African village, or into Edison's or Curie's laboratory, or into Shakespeare's London, or wherever and whenever one wishes. You can go to some lengths supporting the illusion with appropriate equipment, pictures, props, and disguises, or you can be satisfied with stimulating students' imaginations with words alone. Whether or not a teacher goes to the extent of consciously suggesting the notion of the classroom as a place from which one "takes off" into other environments, the implication of this approach is that some sense of the classroom as a time/space machine can relatively easily engage students' imaginations in learning.

I recognize that this suggestion may itself seem a bit exotic to many teachers, and some personalities are more comfortable than others about shaping classroom experience this way. There are no general rules about how to teach, because we all do it differently and have success in various modes that better suit our own personalities and styles of teaching. Nonetheless, the cognitive tools of literacy can be pulled together into a framework that can help planning, whatever style of teaching suits one best.

The Simple Version

Once again, I begin with the simpler form of framework I developed a number of years ago. I am not including this here with the sadistic hope of confusing you with two slightly different frameworks, but just so that you can see how this simpler model incorporates a number of the cognitive tools. Also, even though the more elaborate form of the framework that follows has more support for someone beginning to try this approach, this simpler framework might be referred to as you become familiar with the idea and feel you don't need the more formal framework. And after some time, you will no doubt give up using this one too, no longer needing supports for what has become routine in your planning and teaching.

Second Planning Framework (Simple Version)

1. *Identifying heroic qualities:* What heroic human qualities can be seen and felt as central to the topic? What emotional images do they evoke?
2. *Organizing the content into a narrative structure*
    2.1. *Initial access:* What content, distinct from students' everyday experience, best embodies the heroic qualities most central to the topic? Does this expose some extreme or limit of reality within the topic?
    2.2. *Structuring the body of the unit or lesson:* What content best articulates the topic into a clear narrative structure? Briefly sketch the main narrative line.
    2.3. *Humanizing the content:* How can the content be shown in terms of human hopes, fears, intentions, or other emotions? What aspects of the content can best stimulate romance, wonder, and awe?
    2.4. *Pursuing details:* What content best allows students to pursue some aspect of the topic in exhaustive detail?

3. *Concluding:* How can one best bring the topic to satisfactory closure, while pointing on to further dimensions or to other topics? How can the students *feel* this satisfaction? How can one conclude with a sense of wonder about the topic?
4. *Evaluation:* How can we know whether the topic has been understood and has engaged and stimulated students' imaginations?

Example One: The Industrial Revolution (Ages Thirteen to Fifteen)

The framework may make the lesson-planning task seem formidable, as though it requires teachers to master a complex planning process in place of the more familiar (and thus simple-seeming) procedures they use at present. I hope it will become clear that this model is not so complex as it may at first appear, and that it is in fact a much less artificial way of organizing a topic than the one imposed by the presently dominant procedures. Again, this framework encourages approaching a lesson or unit as a good story to be told rather than as a list of objectives to be attained.

First, then, think about what is heroic about the Industrial Revolution. Any relatively recent social and historical change is infinitely rich in records of events, personalities, artifacts, theories, literature, and so on, and so a major problem for teaching is selection. Traditionally this has stimulated two distinct questions: What bits matter most? What bits will be most meaningful to the particular students? Here, instead, we are asked to think of what is heroic about it and also to reflect on what emotionally strong mental images it conjures.

So what heroic human qualities are embodied in the topic? Most generally, it was a burst of confidence and creative energy such as the world had never seen before. It represents an enormous gamble, hurling the world into vast material transformations, an experimental science generating constant technological innovation, and profound changes in literature, philosophy, and economics that have transformed the face of the earth and cultures all over the world.

Viewed as heroic activity, what is brought to the fore is the sheer energy and (over)confidence that flung the world into a new, and perhaps increasingly terrifying, adventure—and its cost in human suffering. It was a volcanic outburst of energy, power, will. It was the creation of the modern world; we are still living in its wake, still trying to get some control over the titanic forces it unleashed, and still trying to make sense of it and evaluate it.

So the human qualities of energy, courage, and confidence capture something about the heroic nature of the topic. This first overview, however, is merely a perspective; it is not *the* truth.

This first phase of planning is sketched out formally here, even if briefly, but after some practice it should become almost automatic. Once you develop a clear sense of the heroic in various subject areas, then you will be able simply to switch on, as it were, this "heroic" perspective, looking at any topic through that lens. What may seem an academic exercise initially can become a perfectly straightforward, virtually instantaneous, ability, or cognitive tool.

With any complex topic, a wide range of perspectives will be possible, offering an equally wide range of heroic human qualities on which to focus. One could, for example, choose to focus on compassion and dogged persistence, as embodied in the great humanitarian figures of the Industrial Revolution who worked to ameliorate the sufferings of the exploited classes and to stimulate the consciences of the exploiters. One might focus on technical ingenuity, as embodied in the inventors and developers of the tools and machines that provided an engine for the era. One might focus on the heroic resistance of those who have struggled to keep the effects of the Industrial Revolution at bay. One might focus on almost any human quality and allow it to lead to the particular content that best embodies it. Taking a "heroic" perspective, then, is an important first step that will largely determine the range of content to be chosen. You can choose to present the Industrial Revolution as a great triumph of human achievement—or as a vast human disaster, setting us on a destructive course that is poisoning the earth, water, and air and threatening to blow all life and the earth into dark and silent death. The framework, that is, is simply a tool to enable you to make whichever view you choose to present more meaningful and engaging to students.

Let us choose for this example the heroic quality of confident energy and see how this can help in the organization of the content into a narrative structure. The first task is to provide clear access to the topic, engaging students' imaginations with some essential aspect of what the Industrial Revolution is about. In the opening class we will want to form an association between students and a part of the Industrial Revolution that embodies confident energy.

A further characteristic of this approach, and one that runs somewhat counter to the "expanding horizons" principle, is that things strange and remote from students' everyday experience can often be most engaging. So the best opening might be found among content remote from the students' everyday experience, as long as it captures the chosen heroic qualities.

And in addition we must bear in mind here the persistent attraction of narrative. We use principles derived from the story form not simply to entertain students but to communicate the meaning of the unit with maximum emotional clarity and force. We don't have to tie the unit into a simple story form with the tightness appropriate for younger students, but it should still reflect the main principles that give stories their engaging power. Prominent among those is the use of binary opposites. Again, these need not be so prominent as at the earlier stage. Our initial access, then, will set up a dramatic conflict between the embodiment of the heroic human quality of confident energy and whatever opposes it.

In the abstract this perhaps begins to seem impossibly complicated, like keeping four or five balls in the air at once. But if you move back to the example, you'll see how, at the concrete level of planning, things are much more easily dealt with.

Say the first lesson begins with showing students a picture of Isambard Kingdom Brunel. Portrait posters are available, made from photographs taken in 1857. Brunel appears in these pictures as distant indeed from today's students: a small man in a dusty black crumpled suit, a tall top hat, high collar and Victorian bow tie, dangling watch-chain, dirty boots, cigar stuck in the corner of his mouth. He might as well be a Martian as far as modern students' understanding goes. The task is to form an association between the students and Brunel's confident energy.

Behind Brunel in the poster are the enormous chains forged to launch his ship, the *Great Eastern*. Previously the largest iron steamship had been a few hundred tons. Brunel's *Great Eastern* was about twenty-four thousand tons. The first attempt to float it was a disaster. Like all of Brunel's schemes, it bordered on the impossible. It was indeed the limits of the possible that attracted him. These were the great days of heroic engineering, and none was more daring than Brunel. At twenty, he took charge of building the first tunnel under the Thames for the underground railway. Halfway through, he cleared out the debris and held a banquet for the great and famous of London, and further down the tunnel, typical of Brunel, he held an equally grand banquet for his laborers.

He built the Great Western Railway (the G.W.R.—sometimes known as God's Wonderful Railway) from London to Boston (the one in the United States, not the one in England). Well, the railway went out to the west coast of Britain and from there the *Great Eastern* could carry anything on to America. Every mile was a drama. Brunel designed and built some of the most daring and beautiful bridges—including the Clifton Suspension Bridge and the Saltash Bridge. He established the principles that engineers followed for a hundred years, and that formed the model for the Brooklyn Bridge, among so many others. One of the impossibilities he achieved building the G.W.R. was the amazing Box Tunnel—two miles long, on a gradient, half of it through solid rock. It cost many lives and he saw many disasters, but he drove the railway through. On his deathbed, Brunel steamed over the Saltash Bridge. He frightened investors at the time and often had difficulty financing his wild and daring projects.

The teacher might, after a brief discussion of Brunel and his near-impossible engineering feats, invite the students to look again at the portrait and more carefully at his eyes and see something of the confident energy that might reasonably frighten any one of us. He was the Industrial Revolution.

With a few facts and a picture of a dusty little Victorian we can achieve our first step of providing access to the Industrial Revolution by forming an association between our students and the heroic quality of confident energy as embodied in Brunel. One could of course find many other examples to start from. Different teachers might choose a variety of ways of vivifying Brunel's achievements. (Anything from straight exposition to a scripted TV "interview" with Brunel to pretending to be Brunel in person—describing his past and inviting questions from the students—to a dramatization of one particular clash between Brunel and an opponent of some daring scheme could suffice.) What also needs to be made vivid is the opposition to Brunel's confident energy, from investor timidity to natural obstacles.

The next step is to organize the rest of the unit. Overall, we have the requirements of the story form to satisfy. The most prominent binary opposites are given clearly in our opening—between the confident energy of Brunel and the human timidity or natural intractability that opposed the realization of his aims. The main general requirement of the story form is that we must never in our unit simply describe achievements or list statistics or indicate technical innovations; we must in each case show them as products of individuals' confident energy and as having overcome particular obstacles in being realized.

We will include all the usual content that is central to understanding the Industrial Revolution. We will include the opening up of the vast U.S. prairies and their production of meat and grains. This is often presented as sets of statistics with maps indicating increasing cattle range and cultivated land. There is obviously nothing wrong with the statistics and maps, but without a context of vivid, personalized human motives, they tend to remain for students of this age sterile and rather meaningless, and perhaps worst from a historical point of view, inevitable. The students need information about particular ranchers and farmers to bring the statistics to life. (An appropriately written textbook will have such examples readily available.) The expansion of meat and grain production are commonly presented as wonderful achievements, but the abstract statistics are expected to carry the wonder to the students. Students will find it much easier to understand the statistics if they see them as products of heroic human qualities. Individuals exercising those qualities in particular contexts against particular oppositions can better carry the wonder of the achievement that the statistics embody in an abstract way.

The initial access to an essential feature of the Industrial Revolution through Brunel does not end the personalizing. The machines, the meat and grain production, the legislative changes, all need to be seen through the intentions, hopes, fears, and particularly through the confident energy of individuals. Huge ranches and farms did not just happen as though driven by some evolutionary "progress." They were made by individuals against considerable opposition, through their exercise of confident energy, ingenuity, courage, ruthlessness, and so on. And they might have failed.

Another cognitive tool leads us to seek out content exemplifying extremes of human achievement and suffering. The achievements will be dealt with both in the heroic materialism of the age and in the new humanitarianism that developed during this period. We need also, however, to see the opposite pole and consider the extremes of poverty, misery, and exploitation that the Industrial Revolution created. Early on it roused great humanitarian hopes, but it produced, among much else, enormous human suffering. It is important to show these polar opposites not as simply coincidental but as necessarily tied together. The creators and beneficiaries of the Industrial Revolution can easily be presented as merely callous about the suffering they caused, or permitted and benefited from, and no doubt many were. But with students at this age we need to be realistic also in the sense of increasingly "mediating" between the poles of good and bad.

(Perhaps I need to add again that when I talk about the teachers' *showing, presenting, mediating,* and so on, I am using such terms for economy's sake. They don't imply purely teacher-centered exposition—the indicated learning can come as a product of students' explorations or inquiry processes or whatever method seems best able to engage students' imaginations.)

Each of the cognitive tools of Chapter Two can provide guidance in planning units. The interest in extremes, for example, can suggest a class display, or a booklet of Industrial Revolution records. Students could add records that their research uncovers: the deepest mine, the largest ranch, farm, bridge, the most influential invention, the biggest engineering project, the greatest transformation of land, the greatest humanitarian achievement, the biggest disaster, the most workers killed on a single project, and so on.

While organizing the body of the unit, we need to bear in mind the value for students of pursuing some aspects of the topic in exhaustive detail. The teacher might gather resources that would allow this in areas where students might be most readily engaged: Brunel's life, or the lives of Elizabeth Fry or James Watt; the design of steam engines or spinning jennies; making guns with standardized parts; changes in clothing styles; gas lamps, their styles and care, and the lifestyle of lamplighters; dyes and the coloring of the world, and so on.

How should such a unit on the Industrial Revolution conclude? The story line has been the dramatic conflict between confident energy applied to the material world and those forces that opposed it—timidity and fear, the sometimes intransigent material world itself, the forces of conservatism, the skeptical and horrified observers of disrupted social life. The narrative structure requires some kind of resolution of this conflict. And the resolution should open up students' sense of wonder about the Industrial Revolution.

We might present an image of the world as it has been changed by the Industrial Revolution. Look out of almost any window. This world is of a kind undreamed of by those who made it and those who resisted it. It is neither the utopia expected by some nor the nightmare predicted by others. But, whatever we feel about it, the scale of transformation, the heroic activities of building and of organizing immensely complex processes, must be presented in a way that will stimulate students' sense of wonder and awe.

If we have dwelt too much on the confident energy and its products, we can conclude with the images suggested by the poet William Blake of the devouring barbaric technological monster spawned by the Industrial Revolution. We need to convey the aesthetic and moral horror, expressed neatly in Robert Burns's little verse, scratched on a windowpane after viewing the Carron Iron Works in 1787:

> We cam na here to view your works,
> In hopes to be mair wise,
> But only, lest we gang to Hell,
> It may be nae surprise.

The Industrial Revolution is precisely caught in the image of the monster created by Mary Shelley's Victor Frankenstein: human beings made it to further their purposes but it has run amok, cannot be controlled, and terrorizes us. Various methods may be employed to help students achieve some mediation between these polar views. Not least effective would be formal debates, with proponents of each view making their case as vigorously as possible. In conclusion, the class might even draw up a crude list of pros and cons, and consider how one might try to weigh one against the other.

It is most important to make sure that we evaluate what we set out to teach. In this case our purpose is to engage students' imaginations so as to teach an understanding of the Industrial Revolution. A number of standard forms of evaluation can help assess our degree of success in teaching the basic facts and ideas that constitute a part of understanding the Industrial Revolution. We can also use various forms of evaluation of students' imaginative engagement. Some of these can be quite simple, such as keeping records about how much nonrequired reading students do about the topic, how much work they do that goes beyond what is required on projects, and so on. We can also devise ways to assess the imaginativeness of their own work—starting with the joint criteria of unusualness and effectiveness (Barrow, 1988). That is, whatever the students do in the way of required work or involvement in learning should demonstrate effectiveness, in that they show they know and understand the material, but it should also demonstrate some uniqueness, something individual and unusual.

Example Two: Pythagoras's Theorem
(Ages Twelve to Fourteen)

As with many topics for this age range, the essential point is to humanize it. In math and science, this means putting the content much more into the lives of people than is currently normal, bringing out the fact that all the science and math we know was discovered or invented by someone for some human purpose. So, to bring the knowledge back to life for students today, place it in the context of others' lives for whom it had emotional meaning.

First, look for the heroic qualities in Pythagoras's theorem. I have suggested that one way of doing this is to see the topic, in this case the theorem, in the context of the human purposes and emotions of its first discovery. This again suggests a more historical and biographical approach to mathematics than is at present common.

You might usefully start by finding out a little about Pythagoras. Is he the hero of the unit? Any encyclopedia will report that he left his birthplace on the Greek island of Samos and went to found an odd institution that seems to have had something in common with a monastery. At least, he gathered a group of like-minded men and set up his "school" at Crotona in southern Italy. Pythagoras founded and led a sect devoted to the pursuit of knowledge and to a lifestyle that included vegetarianism, secrecy, elaborate rituals, and a worship of Apollo. Pythagoras cultivated *philosophy*, in the sense that has come down to us, as the use of observation and reason to make sense of the world and of experience.

A heroic perspective on the theorem might begin with a discussion of Pythagoras's idea of "the cosmos." It seems it was Pythagoras who first used this concept for an orderly, harmonious, beautiful, and moral whole that encompassed everything. The cosmos was taken to be an organized whole, and the key to that order, the key to understanding the universe, was number. "Number rules the universe," this odd community at Crotona thought. Their passionate belief drove them to intense study of the relationships among numbers, something the surrounding world considered crazy. You might stress the weirdness of this monklike community, leading very strict and disciplined lives focused on seeking the key to the cosmos in an activity people today consider elementary mathematics. The driving ambition of Pythagoras was to show the power of number over the world.

Opening the lesson, you might provide access to this heroic perspective, first, simply by discussing it, and then by showing some of the relationships that fascinated Pythagoras and supported his belief that abstract number could help to make sense of the concrete world. One way of moving from integers to the world was by marking dots for numbers, and building shapes on them. The Pythagoreans would commonly have used sticks to make the dots in carefully groomed sand. Consider the progressions involved here:

If one builds squares on the base numbers and compares those with the triangles, further interesting relationships emerge. If certain sets of numbers are put into particular shapes, yet more remarkable relationships become apparent. Consider a triangle whose sides are built on a ratio of 3:4:5:

Now build a square on each side:

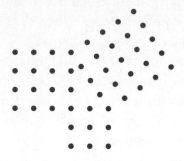

It becomes clear that the number of dots that constitute the square on the hypotenuse are equal to the number of dots that constitute the squares on the other two sides. Nine on the base, plus sixteen on the perpendicular, add up to the twenty-five on the hypotenuse—and so will any other set of integers on an unequal right triangle.

This was triumphant proof to the Pythagoreans that number thus governed geometry, and this was a step in their plan to show that number governed the universe.

The further organization of the lesson might involve joining up the dots into lines and exploring other and more conventional proofs of the theorem. Having embedded discussion of the theorem in the context of the lives of Pythagoras's sect, you can organize the central part of the lesson in a way that teaches the necessary geometrical understanding of Pythagoras's theorem, but in a way that refers back to what was initially so exciting about it.

Opportunities for detailed exploration are many in such a topic. Students might be encouraged to find out what we know about Pythagoras's study of music, and the way numbers were found to govern the scale in ways that remain important to our understanding today. Other topics studied by this group—and their continuing influence in modern thinking—can be studied as well.

The unit can lead to either or both of two conclusions. One concerns the general triumph of Pythagoras's vision, the other its particular failure. The triumph is that people today take for granted what was once a mystical faith and seemingly magical discoveries. The mad sect of Crotona was right and the sane, scornful, hostile world around it was wrong. Mathematics is one of the bases of modern civilization; it is the language of science. All explorations of the cosmos rely on mathematics to a greater or lesser extent. Pythagoras's failure was in the search for harmonious relationships between geometrical shapes and numbers. The proof that the diagonal of a square would not form harmonious relationships with the sides was a severe blow. Pythagoreans referred to this knowledge as "the unutterable." It was a kind of heresy that caused much confusion and distress. This disharmony can be displayed quite easily with dots, particularly when they can be placed with precision, as on a computer. Students should be encouraged by the narrative of the sect's aims to see why this failure caused such distress.

Another kind of conclusion could look at other ancient attempts to apply abstract ideas to the practical world and see some of their results today. Some brief fun might be had discussing Eubulides of Miletus's paradox of the liar and its impact on applying abstract logical reasoning to real events. Consider beginning with the paradox: "A woman says that she is lying. Is what she says true or false?" Sorting out such seemingly trivial problems has taken millennia— and led to the growth of logic and techniques of reasoning, the main steps of which could be explored with students.

Evaluation of such a lesson should include evidence that students understand the theorem and its proof, and also that they understand its importance to the Pythagoreans and how it was a crucial step in applying abstract numbers to the real world.

Adding Depth to the Framework

Now I turn to a more elaborated version of the framework. This version tries to incorporate more of the cognitive tools and also to provide more support for someone trying to use this approach for the first time.

Second Planning Framework (More Supportive Version)

First, a brief sketch:

1. *Identifying heroic qualities:* What heroic human qualities are central to the topic? What emotional images do they evoke? What within the topic can best evoke wonder?

2. *Organizing the topic into a narrative structure:*

    2.1. *Initial access:* What aspect of the topic best embodies the heroic qualities identified as central to the topic? Does this expose some extreme of experience or limit of reality? What image can help capture this aspect?

    2.2. *Composing the body of the lesson or unit:* How do we organize the material into a narrative structure to best illustrate the heroic qualities?

    2.3. *Humanizing the content:* What aspects of the narrative best illustrate the human emotions in it and evoke a sense of wonder? What ideals or challenges to tradition or convention are evident in the content? What humor can we find in the topic?

    2.4. *Pursuing details:* What parts of the topic can students best explore in exhaustive detail?

3. *Concluding:* How can we best bring the topic to satisfactory closure? How can the student feel this satisfaction? How can we evoke a sense of wonder about the topic?

    3.1. *Concluding activity:* What activity might bring the topic home to the students in a meaningful way?

    3.2. *Embryonic forms of theoretic thinking:* How can we encourage the use of some of the cognitive tools that come along with theoretic thinking?

4. *Evaluating:* How can we know that the content has been learned and understood and has engaged and stimulated students' imaginations?

As with the basic elements of the first planning framework, the issues raised by these questions are both deeper and more numerous than in the simple version. The following sections explore each of them in detail before proceeding to further examples.

1. *Identifying Heroic Qualities*. *What heroic human qualities are central to the topic? What emotional images do they evoke? What within the topic can best evoke wonder?*

To help students connect emotionally to the material, teachers need to first identify their own emotional attachment to it. What heroic human quality or emotion—courage, compassion, tenacity, fear, hope, loathing, delight, or whatever—can be found in the topic? These human qualities help teachers, and their students, see the world in human terms and give human meaning to events and ideas in all disciplines. This approach humanizes each topic not to falsify it or to confuse but to infuse the world with human meaning. Again, this first task is the most difficult part of planning the lesson or unit. You are asked to *feel* about the topic as well as to think about it; indeed, you are asked to "perfink" (David Kresch's term for perceiving, feeling, and thinking together) about it.

Things to List:

- Identifying heroic qualities:
- Main heroic quality:
- Alternatives:
- Images that capture the heroic quality:

---

2. *Organizing the Topic into a Narrative Structure*. This process has four steps:

2.1. Initial Access. *What aspect of the topic best embodies the heroic qualities identified as central to the topic? Does this expose some extreme of experience or limit of reality? What image can help capture this aspect?*

For the first lesson of a unit or the opening part of a single lesson, teachers are asked to search their own imagination for images that catch the heroic quality that will provide the dramatic structure for the unit. Remember, it is as important to *feel* the heroic qualities as well as to *think* about them.

2.2. Composing the Body of the Lesson or Unit. How do we organize the material into a narrative structure to best illustrate the heroic qualities?

Sketch the story, ensuring that the qualities will be made clear by the narrative. The principal heroic quality should provide the drama and conflict in the story. Remember, the heroic qualities should be those that most effectively convey the content of the topic.

Things to List:

• Overall structure of the lesson or unit:

2.3. Humanizing the Content. What aspects of the narrative best illustrate the human emotions in it and evoke a sense of wonder? What ideals or challenges to tradition or convention are evident in the content? What humor can you find in the topic?

Think of how a good movie or novel makes aspects of the world engaging. Obstacles to the hero are humanized in one form or another, almost given motives; they are seen in human terms. To do this, you don't need to falsify anything, you simply highlight a particular way of seeing it—because this is precisely the way students' imaginations are engaged by knowledge.

Things to List:

• Content to show in terms of hopes, fears, intentions, or other emotions:

2.4. Pursuing Details. What parts of the topic can students best explore in exhaustive detail?

While it is easy to give students a project to carry out, it is a little harder to think about what aspect of the topic they might be able to *exhaust*, that is, be able to find out nearly everything that is known about it. But there are such parts in every topic, and the security and sense of mastery that come from knowing nearly as much as anyone about something are a great stimulus to inquiry. Think of something that is intriguing, that can be seen from a variety of different perspectives, or that is alluded to but not examined in detail in the content or in your teaching of it. (Referring to your notes from sections 2.2 and 2.3 should help!)

3. Concluding. *How can we best bring the topic to satisfactory closure? How can the student feel this satisfaction? How can we evoke a sense of wonder about the topic?*

3.1. Concluding Activity. What activity might bring the topic home to the students in a meaningful way?

It is good to end a topic in a heroic way, which can have two forms. The first form is to reexamine the initial images and review the content through the lenses of other heroic qualities, including some that might give an opposite or conflicting image to that of the earlier choice. The second form is to show how the romantic association the students have formed can help them understand other topics in a new way. Or you can use both, of course. In concluding you will also want to reflect back on the topic, bringing out why people should feel wonder or awe about it.

Things to List:

• Concluding activities:

3.2. Embryonic Forms of Theoretic Thinking. How can we encourage the use of some of the cognitive tools that come along with theoretic thinking?

Throughout the period during which the tools of literacy are developing, teachers will also see examples of some of their students being attracted by some of the tools to be discussed in the next chapter—cognitive tools that focus on theoretic issues and interests. Signs of these embryonic tools will include students' ready use of general ideas and terms—"society," "evolution," and causal reasoning, abstract moral considerations, and so on. It will not be difficult to provide such students, and the others, with some exercise of philosophical ideas and theoretical issues.

Things to List:

• Further cognitive tools that can encourage theoretic thinking:

---

4. Evaluating. *How can we know that the content has been learned and understood and has engaged and stimulated students' imaginations?*

Any of the traditional forms of evaluation can be used, but in addition, teachers might want to get some measure of how far students' imaginations have been engaged by the topic, how far they have successfully made an imaginative engagement with the material. In addition, the concluding exercises can also be evaluative in nature. Students could be asked to identify heroic qualities in stories in other disciplines to examine both their imaginative use of narrative and their understanding of the content. Heroic qualities can also be examined in moral and ethical terms.

Things to List:

• Forms of evaluation to be used:

Example Three: Parallel Lines Cut by a Transversal Form Congruent Alternate Interior Angles (Ages Eight to Fifteen)

Here's another example from mathematics, which might seem the hardest area in which to design humanized narratives. Say your local curriculum requires you to teach the theorem: "Parallel lines cut by a transversal form congruent alternate interior angles." How can the framework help in organizing this topic so that it will be imaginatively engaging to students? I'll use the framework and lay it out category by category and see what emerges.

1. Identifying Heroic Qualities. *What heroic human qualities are central to the topic? What emotional images do they evoke? What within the topic can best evoke wonder?*

What heroic human quality or emotion hides in this geometry theorem? That is, how can anyone *feel* anything about congruent alternate interior angles? Not exactly a topic to set the blood pounding. Nonetheless, with a bit of thought, it's almost always possible to locate some human source that can bring the topic to imaginative life. One heroic quality evident in this task comes from the practical ingenuity involved in using this theorem to measure the circumference of the earth, and this is best shown in the work of the person who first managed it with remarkable accuracy—the ancient Greek, Eratosthenes of Cyrene, head of the great library at Alexandria.

Main heroic quality: Practical ingenuity.

Alternatives: The power of a simple theorem to achieve an astonishing result.

Images that capture the heroic quality: What in the world connected with congruent alternate interior angles can evoke the sense of practical ingenuity? I see Eratosthenes, the venerable director of the library at Alexandria, very carefully erecting a rod in a pit in a courtyard of the library, ensuring that it is exactly vertical, and then measuring the angle of the shadow cast by the sun at noon. What he is doing, with this simple tool, is calculating the circumference of the earth.

2. Organizing the Topic into a Narrative Structure. This process has four steps:

2.1 Initial Access. What aspect of the topic best embodies the heroic qualities identified as central to the topic? Does this expose some extreme of experience or limit of reality? What image can help to capture this aspect?

Images that catch the heroic quality of the geometry theorem will provide the dramatic structure for the unit. Rather than focus exclusively on the content and how to organize it, look at your own understanding of the topic and its content and search your imagination for those images that best capture what is important about it. Anything extreme or exotic will usually provide a good starting point, as long as it captures the heroic quality identified as a central organizing feature of the unit.

Exotic or extreme content that best embodies the heroic quality: Initial access to the topic might usefully be provided in this case by introducing the students to the formidable polymath Eratosthenes of Cyrene (who lived around 275–194 B.C.). He was one of those omnivorous inquirers with a distinct practical bent, in the style of Leonardo da Vinci. He did significant work in astronomy, history, literary criticism (including a twelve-volume work, *On Ancient Comedy*), philosophy, poetry, and mathematics. He also devised a calendar, with leap years. He calculated the distances of the moon and the sun from the earth, though not as accurately as his calculation of the earth's circumference. In old age he became blind and, so the story goes, voluntarily starved himself to death. Such an introduction also can catch at some extremes of reality and experience. We will, then, structure the body of this unit by beginning with Eratosthenes's method of calculating the circumference of the earth, seeing the theorem ingeniously applied to a practical problem.

2.2. Composing the Body of the Lesson or Unit. How do we organize the material into a narrative structure to best illustrate the heroic qualities?

The basic narrative structure here is tied up with the method that Eratosthenes used to calculate the circumference of the earth by means of the theorem under study.

Overall structure of the lesson or unit: How did Eratosthenes use the theorem to calculate the earth's circumference using a vertical rod in Alexandria? Five hundred miles to the south of Alexandria, on what we call the Tropic of Cancer, was the town of Syene, on the site of present-day Aswan. (This calculation works out more neatly in miles than in kilometers.) Eratosthenes knew that at noon on the summer solstice in Syene a vertical rod cast no shadow. He also knew that the sun was very distant from the earth and that its rays could be considered as striking different places on the earth in parallel. So to the image. Around 200 B.C. Eratosthenes mounted a vertical rod in Alexandria, and at noon on the summer solstice he measured the angle its shadow cast. From that measurement he calculated with remarkable accuracy, by means of the target theorem, the circumference of the earth. How?

Consider this diagram:

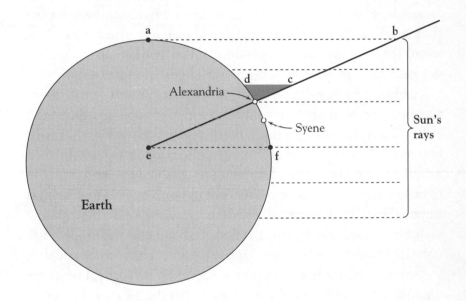

From the theorem, Eratosthenes (with whose name students should obviously become familiar—and be able to pronounce accurately) knew that <ABE and <BEF in this diagram are congruent alternate interior angles—that is, whatever <ABE is, <BEF will be the same. By holding a pole upright in Alexandria, he held it along the line EB. The top of the pole forms <ECD, which is also

congruent with <ABE and <BEF. Eratosthenes's careful measurement of the angle of the shadow at noon—<ECD—yielded 7 degrees 12 minutes. That meant that <BEF must also be 7 degrees 12 minutes. This distance is about 1/50 of the 360 degrees of a full circle, and so the distance from Alexandria to Syene was 1/50 of the circumference of the earth. Multiplying 50 times 500 gave 25,000, so the circumference of the earth must be about 25,000 miles—which it is.

2.3. Humanizing the Content. What aspects of the story best illustrate the human emotions in it and evoke a sense of wonder? What ideals or challenges to tradition or convention are evident in the content?

The framework suggests thinking of how a good movie or novel makes aspects of the world engaging. It isn't hard to imagine how the narrative about Eratosthenes could be made into a movie—it seems made for dramatic presentation. Well, perhaps an interesting documentary, anyway; it lacks obvious shoot-'em-up possibilities.

Content to show in terms of hopes, fears, intentions or other emotions: Eratosthenes's revolutionary ideas can be set against the convention that accepts the unknown as unknowable, that feels fear in the face of whatever is beyond the boundary of established norms and routines. The ideal he represents is the determined use of practical ingenuity to achieve what to the conventional mind is impossible. His ingenuity is tied to his passionate desire to know about the world. He represents an ideal that can attract the imagination of students at this age. They are beginning to recognize that we are here on earth for a small time, and we can accept what we are told about it or we can use our minds in the great adventure of discovering the nature of our peculiar world and our odd minds' experience of it. Eratosthenes is heroic in the sense that he shows how practical ingenuity can disclose what might otherwise be considered impossible to know.

2.4. Pursuing Details. What parts of the topic can students best explore in exhaustive detail?

Aspects of the topic that students can explore exhaustively: In this case, the students can take part in a repetition of Eratosthenes's discovery. All they need is an Internet connection with a school a known distance to the south of theirs and a stick they can erect, on a sunny day, exactly vertical, and then some means of measuring the angle of the shadow it casts. While it is easier to work out with cities on or in the tropics, this method will still work with any two cities distant from each other but on much the same longitude. Teachers in, say, Toronto and Miami, or Calgary and Phoenix, or Melbourne and Cooktown, could arrange to measure the angle cast by the sun at noon on particular days, compare figures, and, with slight modification, use Eratosthenes's method to calculate the earth's circumference.

Small groups of students could also explore all that is known about the great library at Alexandria, or about Eratosthenes himself. Students can discover the whole of human knowledge about these exotic topics in quite a short time of intensive exploration. They could also explore the lives and achievements of other mathematicians at the time. Or compare Eratosthenes's measures of the earth with the much less accurate ones reported by Ptolemy. (Ptolemy's became the more widely believed—which is why Columbus thought he had reached Asia when he landed in the Caribbean.)

Some students might make a collection of Ancient Mathematician cards, on the model of the baseball or hockey cards devoted to star players. This might provide some exercise and fun on computers, finding images for the front and their achievements and "records" for the back.

3. Concluding. *How can we best bring the topic to satisfactory closure? How can the student feel this satisfaction?*

3.1. Concluding Activity. What activity might bring the topic home to the students in a meaningful way?

Concluding activities: It's essential to convey how Eratosthenes exemplifies a magus-like cleverness. He did not need to travel around the world, measuring distance in the conventional ways. Using the ingenious techniques of geometry—a kind of magic too casually taken for granted now—he was able to calculate the earth's circumference to within a few miles at a time when most of its inhabitants had no idea even that it was round. Teachers would do well to work at bringing to the fore the awe, wonder, and romance of geometry, rather than presenting it as a set of routine, taken-for-granted techniques to be learned. By associating with Eratosthenes's ingenuity in calculating distances to the moon and sun, and the earth's circumference, by extending from the slim base of the geometric theorem that was already known, one can help students become engaged by what is remarkable and wonderful about geometry. Geometry, and mathematics in general, can thus be seen not just as an endless set of algorithms and theorems but as a romantic adventure. Closely looking at the theorem, at how its simple magic works to produce such astonishing knowledge, can help convey something of the wonder of geometry.

3.2. Embryonic Forms of Theoretic Thinking. How can we encourage the use of some of the cognitive tools that come along with theoretic thinking?

Further cognitive tools that can encourage theoretic thinking: We can summarize what is known about Eratosthenes's life, and that of other Greek geometers, and ask why geometry developed so explosively among the Greeks and arithmetic hardly at all. How was it connected with Egyptian needs to measure land accurately, and why did the Egyptians need to develop these skills? What uses was geometry put to in their temple building? These questions, and whatever materials teachers can make available, might all serve as useful stimuli to theoretic thinking.

4. Evaluating. *How can we know that the content has been learned and understood and has engaged and stimulated students' imaginations?*

Forms of evaluation to be used: Traditional forms of evaluation can reveal whether students understand the geometric principle and can apply it to new cases. In addition, look for evidence that students have associated in some degree with the quality of practical ingenuity that Eratosthenes has exemplified. A difficulty with looking for precise measures of such qualities is that they may take different forms in each individual's behavior. But the observant teacher would be able to use practical ingenuity to measure whether or not, or the degree to which, students find the discovery of congruence in alternate interior angles imaginatively engaging. At the simplest level, their enthusiasm would provide an index, as would their interest in learning about mathematicians and geometers contemporary with Eratosthenes, such as Archimedes, Nicomedes, and others—subjects for the class set of Ancient Mathematician cards! Involvement in reading or other work about the topic beyond what has been required by the teacher will also signal imaginative engagement.

Example Four: The Life Cycle of a Cold-Blooded Vertebrate (Ages Eight to Ten)

Heroic quality in a cold-blooded vertebrate? Let's take the eel as the subject for this unit, and see how the framework helps shape the topic for imaginative teaching and learning.

1. Identifying Heroic Qualities. *What heroic human qualities are central to the topic? What emotional images do they evoke? What within the topic can best evoke wonder?*

What heroic human quality or emotion—courage, compassion, tenacity, fear, hope, loathing, delight, or whatever—can be found in the topic of eels? These qualities help teachers—and students—see the world in human terms and give human meaning to events, facts, and ideas in all disciplines.

Main heroic quality: Scientists' ingenious persistence in uncovering the life cycle of the eel.

Alternative: Astonishing journeying of the eel.

Images that capture the heroic quality: The Danish scientist Johannes Schmidt criss-crossed the Atlantic on the decks of various ships from Iceland to the Canary Islands, from North Africa to North America, pulling endless catches aboard and examining their contents in his unrelenting attempt to unravel the mystery of the life cycle of eels. He began his search in 1904 and continued for twenty years, suspending his voyages reluctantly during the First World War. His unremarked voyages, single-mindedly pursuing knowledge about eels, challenge those of legendary Sinbads or Jasons, and those of Drake, Magellan, and Cook. And what was he doing all those years, braving the Atlantic Ocean in all weathers? He was looking for younger and younger eels, elvers, larvae, and tracing them by age in order to locate their breeding grounds.

2. *Organizing the Topic into a Narrative Structure.* This process has four steps:

2.1. Initial Access. What aspect of the topic best embodies the heroic qualities identified as central to the topic? Does this expose some extreme of experience or limit of reality?

The mystery of eels' sex lives makes a good place to begin. In the ancient world much knowledge had already been accumulated about all kinds of creatures, but eels presented a bizarre mystery. Eels were very common, but no one had ever found a baby eel or even a pregnant eel. The Egyptians, Greeks, and Romans considered eels a delicacy, yet despite becoming expert at catching them, they discovered virtually nothing about their life cycle. Aristotle proposed that the eel was sexless and that its young were created spontaneously out of the mud in river bottoms. Pliny suggested that when they wanted to procreate, eels rubbed themselves against rocks, and young were formed from the skin thus detached. Other explanations of their birth included that they come from putrefying material in rivers, that they come from the gills of other fishes, that they grew from horses' hairs that dropped into water, or delightfully, that they were sinful monks whom St. Dunstan in a rage had transformed to do eternal penance (so giving the English cathedral town of Ely its name—the eely place).

2.2. Composing the Body of the Lesson or Unit. How do we organize the material into a story to best illustrate the heroic qualities?

Overall structure of the lesson or unit: The solution of a 2,500-year-old mystery, solved only in the twentieth century through the heroic, persistent ingenuity of Johannes Schmidt. At the end of the nineteenth century, a tiny, transparent, leaflike fish, quite unlike an eel, was caught in the western Mediterranean. A few similar specimens had been seen before and designated a new genus. This particular specimen was reared in a fish tank, and by a series of amazing transformations grew into an elver and then into an adult eel. (The larvae are called *leptocephali*—another word for students to learn.) But if eels were so common, why were specimens of eel larvae so very rare? This opens up a historical perspective on the unraveling of the eel's life cycle, though each new discovery only seems to leave further puzzles; Schmidt becomes heroic through the ingenuity and persistence he displays in tracing the early life of the eel. It might be useful to set off Schmidt's voyages and discoveries against the social and political background of his time, which absorbed most people's attention. While the politicians and soldiers filled center stage, wreaking the terrible destruction of the First World War, Schmidt's gradual piecing together of the eel's life cycle contributed something small to our accumulating knowledge. The counterpointing of his slow, persistent inquiry against the cataclysmic destruction that fills our history texts might lead to brief meditations on the value of different kinds of activities, and so stimulate some wonder.

The narrative will follow Schmidt's early explorations in the Mediterranean. He discovered more larvae and found that on average they were larger in size the further east they were caught. So he sailed out into the Atlantic, finding ever-smaller larvae drifting in the currents. Schmidt persuaded more than twenty ship-owners to collect samples for him, and to chart where each was found. He began to home in on the area where the greatest concentrations of tiny larvae were found, locating their breeding ground between latitudes 20 and 30 degrees North and longitudes 50 and 65 degrees West, among the strange floating weeds that constitute the Sargasso Sea.

2.3. Humanizing the Content. What aspects of the story best illustrate the human emotions in it and evoke a sense of wonder? What ideals or challenges to tradition or convention are evident in the content?

Content to show in terms of hopes, fears, intentions, or other emotions: A sense of romance can be caught up in the details of Schmidt's voyages and discoveries, in the dedication, the ingenuity, the persistence, the endless miles of the Atlantic traversed in search of tiny larvae. Wonder can be stimulated by the strange life cycle gradually uncovered; the floating larvae carried on currents for months or years and for up to three or four thousand miles, their bizarre transformation from larvae to elvers, their finding—for thousands of years that we know of—the same rivers of Europe and America, their peculiar sexual progress from neuter, to precocious feminization, to hermaphrodite, before settling for male or female conditions, their unfailing migration back to the sea after about ten years in their freshwater home rivers. Awe might be stimulated by just considering the purpose of all this remarkable complexity in eels' life cycle. Why? Perhaps compare their life cycle and travels with those of the students in the class and their reasons for the typical patterns of travel they and their siblings and parents engage in. Why, again?

2.4. Pursuing Details. What parts of the topic can students best explore in exhaustive detail?

Aspects of the topic that students can explore exhaustively: This topic provides a wealth of details that might be fairly exhaustively pursued—charting the changes from larva to elver; the foods of eels at various stages of life; Schmidt's voyages; the variety of forms of larvae, from threadlike to saucerlike forms, and the adult forms they grow into; the families of eels; the Sargasso Sea, and so on. For the keen "baseball" card makers, here's an opportunity for a set of cards of the most famous eels—"collect them all!"

3. Concluding. *How can we best bring the topic to satisfactory closure? How can the student feel this satisfaction? How can we evoke a sense of wonder about the topic?*

3.1. Concluding Activity. *What activity might bring the topic home to the students in a meaningful way?*

Concluding activities: You might provide in conclusion a different narrative, this time bringing together the sequential outline of the eel's life cycle, from Sargasso Sea to American and European rivers and back again. This telling might highlight those aspects of the life cycle that are still not known or understood. We still lack, for example, a clear image of how male and female eels reproduce in the Sargasso Sea. We do not know how many of, or even whether, the European eels who set off on their long migration back to the Sargasso Sea ever make it. We do not know the mechanisms that trigger and guide their migrations. You might connect this with other creatures with exotic migration patterns—salmon, birds, butterflies, and so on.

3.2. Embryonic Forms of Theoretic Thinking. *How can we encourage the use of some of the cognitive tools that come along with theoretic thinking?*

Further cognitive tools that can encourage theoretic thinking: Ask students to think of the intricacies of the relationships between life forms on our planet and their often strange interactions. What do eels eat, and what eats eels? A good day is one in which we eat and are not eaten—or at least that is what moves most of the life forms on our planet. What are the main theories about strange migration patterns?

4. Evaluating. *How can we know that the content has been learned and understood and has engaged and stimulated students' imaginations?*

Forms of evaluation to be used: Various methods can be used to evaluate a unit such as this, to confirm that students have learned in detail about eels and their life cycle, and also that they know which features of eels' lives remain mysterious. Traditional forms of evaluation can reveal students' knowledge—tests, written work, projects, and so on.

Because the goal has been to engage students' imaginations with eels, it's also important to evaluate success in this regard.

Obviously, teachers don't have well-tried and tested evaluation procedures that will give precise readings of imaginative engagement, and probably never will have. But you might experiment with plausible ways of getting some kind of reading—perhaps beginning, simply, with observation. It is usually fairly clear whether or not students are imaginatively engaged in a topic; the degree of their enthusiasm, the way it invades their intellectual activity in general, their pursuit of aspects of it well beyond what is required, their questioning and searching out additional sources of information, their desire simply to talk about it, are all indicators of some degree of imaginative engagement. Students' written work, or other forms in which they present what they have learned to the teacher or to the class as a whole, can yield evidence of imaginative engagement; going beyond what is required, especially when the direction has been determined by the student's perhaps idiosyncratic interests, or taking great care in, for example, drawing different forms of larvae or species of eel, or evidence of knowledge that has been culled from diverse sources not readily available, or evidence of a kind of obsessive interest in some feature of eels' lives, would provide some indication of imaginative engagement. Some of these characteristics of student work could, of course, be due to other factors, like desire for a high grade or compulsion. But it is an unusually unobservant teacher who cannot tell the difference. These points echo in brief ideas that are elaborated and developed in Eisner's "connoisseurship" model of evaluation (1985).

Example Five: Trees (Ages Twelve to Fifteen)

The growing concern about environmental issues —makes topics like this one—"Trees"—likely to appeal to students. This example is oriented toward the upper end of the age range, and its narrative structure includes some general ideas designed to help carry students into the kind of understanding central to the following chapters.

1. *Identifying Heroic Qualities.* *What heroic human qualities are central to the topic? What emotional images do they evoke? What within the topic can best evoke wonder?*

How can you identify heroic human qualities in trees? We think of trees as providing our chief building materials and fuel (remembering also that coal is made from trees that decayed during the lush Carboniferous period); they yield pulp for paper; they produce edible fruits and nuts; they give off the oxygen we require for life and absorb the carbon dioxide we exhale; their roots conserve water and prevent soil erosion; and they provide homes for a vast array of animals and insects. Trees are thus crucial to human life, to the structure of our world, and to the fabric of our civilization. So you might choose as a usable transcendent quality faithful supportiveness. That is, you will present trees in terms of the faithful support they have constantly given to human beings and human civilizations. (Yes, this is anthropomorphizing; as far as anyone knows, trees don't have the emotional machinery to feel in that fashion. Nonetheless, students of this age have the capacity to impute such feelings—and will absorb the lessons more effectively when they do so.) One of the themes to be brought out by this choice will be how people respond to this faithful support.

This whole introductory theme has within it an expression of extreme behaviors—greed going so far as to undermine what supplies its desires. It expresses the same moral as the story of killing the goose that laid the golden eggs.

Main heroic quality: Faithful supporters.

Alternatives: Incredible diversity.

Images that capture the heroic quality: If we consider the prolific diversity of trees and their appearance around the world in endless shapes and sizes, and how people, poets in particular, use them to represent human moods—the tranquil peace of a tall tree on a summer's evening, the riotous anger of windswept trees, and so on—and how they supply ideal building materials and fruit and so many other constituents of our civilizations, we find them tangled in every aspect of our lives and history. An image that catches some of this, quite a common image in the Middle Ages, is one in which we see our different cultures through the ages and across the world nestled in the branches of some great tree. Closely related cultures spread across individual branches; the trunk can be Time; more recent cultures are growing in the canopy, enjoying the sun of the present. Each culture can be seen using the tree—to build, to carve, to make utensils, to burn—(with its obvious dangers)—and some do greater or lesser damage to the great tree. Nonetheless lives of every culture—kind or cruel—depend on it. As teachers, we can encourage our students to elaborate the image to whatever extent seems useful.

2. Organizing the Topic into a Narrative Structure. This process has four steps:

2.1. Initial Access. What aspect of the topic best embodies the heroic qualities identified as central to the topic? Does this expose some extreme of experience or limit of reality? What image can help capture this aspect?

Content that best embodies the heroic quality: To provide students with initial access to the topic, it is useful to introduce content that is distinct from their everyday experience but catches the transcendent quality intended in the narrative. One way of doing this might be to have students look at human civilizations in what may initially seem a rather odd way. That is, to see the growth of civilizations as based on exploitation of the faithful supportiveness of trees, and the decline of civilizations as caused by excessive exploitation exhausting the supply.

2.2. Composing the Body of the Lesson or Unit. How do we organize the material into a narrative structure to best illustrate the heroic qualities?

Overall structure of the lesson or unit: You can take just the familiar outline narrative of Western history and recast it in a quite different light, or take a new perspective on it. Thus the Sumerian kingdom of Mesopotamia can be seen as owing much of its wealth to learning how to exploit its great cedar trees. After nearly a thousand years, the Sumerian civilization came to an ignominious end due to overvigorous logging. Salts eroded from the denuded hills and ruined the fruitful agricultural valleys.

In similar vein, the rise and fall of all the ancient civilizations can be traced in terms of their access to trees. Athens rose on the power it gained through ships produced from the forests of Attica, and fell as that reliable source of timber was destroyed by the Spartans during the Peloponnesian War. The Roman Empire collapsed as it could no longer support its legions in the North and East. That support relied very heavily on silver from Spanish mines. The silver was not exhausted, but it could no longer be smelted because the Roman furnaces had consumed 500 million trees and laid waste seven thousand square miles of productive forest. The burst of Tudor economic development, and the basis for England's maritime empire, was laid by Robert Cecil's giving trading monopolies only to English-built ships. This led to the rapid depletion of oak forests for shipbuilding, but it also stimulated related activities such as glassblowing and iron smelting. Through the following couple of centuries, the forested island of Britain was laid almost bare. In three decades around the Civil War (in the middle of the seventeenth century), the ten-thousand-hectare Forest of Dean was reduced to just a couple of hundred trees. Britain's fate did not so quickly follow that of earlier empires only because of the invention of the coking process for coal and the rise of steam power. Similarly, the United States, "an almost universal forest" as a French visitor described it shortly after Independence, saw its woodlands fuel the needs of farmers and burgeoning industry, of steamships and railroads. Coal, again, saved American economic and political power for some time.

Thus the rise and fall of the civilizations of the ancient and early modern worlds can generally be told in terms of their exploitation and exhaustion of timber. And today, economic growth in many Third World countries is still being fueled by the consumption of their forests. What is being done in the Amazon is being done in British Columbia, and has been done throughout the ages. Trees have faithfully supported the growth of civilizations, and those who have abused this faithful support have been destroyed as a result. Perhaps we are now seeing this same cycle on a planetary scale. In such a context it becomes a bit futile for the wealthy countries, whose power was gained by exploiting and destroying their own forests, to lecture Third World countries who are only following that example.

What clear narrative structure will be best for building knowledge about trees? You could develop the opening theme and follow a historical outline, looking at the different trees used in different civilizations and the varied purposes they were used for. This would focus the class on the characteristics of various trees, their typical environmental conditions, the qualities of their woods, the varied uses made of them—from building to fuel to toys to art. That is, I think it would be possible to use the dramatic and unconventional tree-centered view of history as a workable narrative structure. To do this adequately, however, would require more information than many teachers have at their fingertips.

If I had to plan such a unit with my own limited knowledge of trees, I might prefer a different narrative structure, one that will focus students on a more general range of knowledge of trees and their faithful supportiveness. As faithful supportiveness is the chosen transcendent quality, it will need to be foremost in the narrative. At its simplest, I could consider the range of ways in which trees are faithfully supportive. But the narrative needs some principle that will give a sense of coherent and meaningful movement through that range. If all inspiration fails, something like size would do, beginning with the smallest trees and the ways they are faithfully supportive to whichever people, gradually working up to the biggest trees and their uses. Or you could move from the hardest woods to the softest, or follow scientific classifications of trees.

A bit better, however, would be a narrative structure that has a central affective component. Trees might be seen as involved in struggles between conditions that favor their growth and spread, and those that threaten them. It is clear where the humans they faithfully support would feature in this scenario. Alternatively, a narrative structured by the degrees of trees' faithful supportiveness to humans could work. You could even take a scheme like Maslow's "hierarchy of needs" (1970) and show how trees contribute to each need—from oxygen for life itself to toys or equipment for our self-fulfilling play. You might pick up the historical theme from the introduction and look at the contributions of trees to human life from the earliest food and construction materials to the most modern. The narrative choice will be determined by the requirement that students learn about the biology of trees, their variety, and their environmental roles.

The affective component, however, can be injected by responding to the remaining questions in the framework, even if the narrative structure is as stark as moving from the roots of the tree and working up the trunk to the branches and foliage. You could concentrate on each in turn, considering the variety of forms in different trees, and build your unit around the faithful supportiveness of each part. I'll take this simple narrative structure for the rest of the sample unit.

So the students will see the tree, like any living thing, designed to reproduce itself. The roots hold it in place and get the required nutrients, the trunk is to raise the reproductive parts and expose them to pollination and the leaves to light for photosynthesis. The trunk also moves water and other nutrients up and moves food down to the roots for storage and for use as growth tissue.

2.3. Humanizing the Content. What aspects of the narrative best illustrate the human emotions in it and evoke a sense of wonder? What ideals or challenges to tradition or convention are evident in the content?

Content to show in terms of hopes, fears, intentions, or other emotions: Begin by considering how the content can be shown in terms of human hopes, fears, intentions, and other emotions. In the case of trees I think this is rather easy, especially given the basic transcendent quality that is directing the focus here. Students will learn about root systems and trunks and leaves and fruit in terms of the ways they support various human hopes, fears, intentions, and so on. This can be made easier by using case studies occasionally. Consider, for example, a tribe whose life is intricately bound up with the fruit and wood products derived from particular trees.

What aspects of the content can best stimulate romance, wonder, and awe? It would take a considerable amount of knowledge about trees to respond to this question fully. Romance and wonder can be stimulated by knowledge of the strangest or most exotic trees, by peculiar life cycles or extreme attainments. Students might, again, compile a "book of records" noting the Pacific Coast redwoods as the tallest trees, reaching over 105 meters; the giant sequoias as the most massive; the Japanese-trained bonsai (of many genera and species) as the smallest; the Mexican swamp cypress extending to 50 meters in circumference; the bristlecone pines in Nevada being the oldest living things on earth, reaching 4,600 years; and the double cocoanut that is native to a couple of tiny islands in the Seychelles, whose fruit takes ten years to mature and reaches twenty kilos in weight. One can look at the oddest trees, like the mangrove, the South American ombu, the Madagascar traveler's tree, or the talipot palm of Asia—which grows steadily for about seventy-five years and then bursts into glorious flower and dies. Students might discover how many seeds a young pine gives off in a year or the number of species of flowering trees in the world. They can also get busy with another set of cards if they want.

While studying the trunk, one might wonder at the workability of wood, considering the remarkable technology developed to respond to this central feature of trees' faithful supportiveness—at the tools for cutting and shaping wood, drying it and treating it against decay, the endless ingenious fastening devices, screws, and nails that help to restructure wood into new shapes and purposes. Awe might be encouraged by asking each student to write a one-year biography of a particular tree. During that time they could produce a book with photographs, measurements, poems, information, and drawings of "their" tree.

It may seem obvious that one can readily locate ideals and revolts against conventions in this topic. The realization of the exhaustibility of trees, the destruction of species, the elimination of forests, and the impact of all this on the ecosystem provides an ideal of conservation and good management of trees, one that runs counter to the convention of thoughtless exploitation that has prevailed for so long. The historical introduction laid the ground for this on the basis of simple self-interest. But the ideal may take students beyond self-interest toward an ideal of shared life: trees were not made for us; we share a planet, and ideally our lives contribute to each other's. The relationship between trees and humans is distinctly unequal. They need us much less than we need them. Though such a perspective might better come in the section about encouraging theoretic cognitive tools.

But another, unconventional, way of seeing trees in revolt against conventions could be to consider their long resistance to classification. This begins with the inability to give a precise definition of *tree*. There is such a gradual change from the paradigmatic trees to shrubs to herbaceous plants that one cannot draw a clear line. The problems continue with attempts to classify kinds of trees. General distinctions between softwoods (conifers) and hardwoods (dicotyledons) become distinctly unuseful when balsa, the softest of all woods, shows up as a hardwood. "Evergreen" and "deciduous" turn out to be less than useful categories when some species retain their foliage in winter or lose it depending on climatic conditions. In the process of studying the greater or lesser adequacy of various classificatory schemes in this context, students should learn a considerable amount about the various terms and names given to kinds of trees.

2.4. Pursuing Details. What parts of the topic can students best explore in exhaustive detail?

Aspects of the topic that students can explore exhaustively: The pursuit of detailed knowledge about some particular tree, or parts of a tree, or process of growth, or whatever, can be given to small groups of students for the period of the unit. One might give them the long-term task of writing and illustrating a one-year biography of a tree. The aim is to enable students to develop as exhaustive as possible an understanding of some aspect of the topic, to give them a sense of the security that can come with knowing as much about something as anyone in the world.

3. Concluding. *How can we best bring the topic to satisfactory closure? How can the student feel this satisfaction? How can we evoke a sense of wonder about the topic?*

3.1. Concluding Activity. What activity might bring the topic home to the students in a meaningful way?

Concluding activities: An excellent conclusion for this unit would be to tell or read or watch the animated film of Jean Giorno's *The Man Who Planted Trees*. Giorno tells of his walking as a young man in a desolate region in the south of France and eventually, worried about lack of water and food, meeting a shepherd. During the evening the shepherd carefully sorted a dozen acorns, and the next day he planted them. Giorno stayed a few days, and each day the shepherd planted more acorns. The story of Elzéard Bouffier, the shepherd, covers forty years, during which, interrupted by wars and his own marriage and family life, Giorno occasionally revisits him. Over the years of planting trees, woods sprout and grow and eventually forests thrive. They retain water, and so streams flow again where earlier there had long been dry beds, and people come back to the deserted villages and rebuild. Bouffier, by slowly planting trees day by day, brought back thronging life to what had been a rocky desert. (The Canadian Film Board animated film, available on VHS and DVD, won an Oscar for its vivid recreation of the story.)

3.2. Embryonic Forms of Theoretic Thinking. How can we encourage the use of some of the cognitive tools that come along with theoretic thinking?

Further cognitive tools that can encourage theoretic thinking: In this case I have built in a number of inducements to theoretic thinking along the way. The very notion of viewing human history with trees' playing the central role is an invitation to theoretic thinking.

4. Evaluating. *How can we know that the content has been learned and understood and has engaged and stimulated students' imaginations?*

Forms of evaluation to be used: Once again, you can use whatever traditional evaluation procedures seem appropriate to discover whether students have learned the basic knowledge concerning trees. You will also want to observe their work on the biography of "their" tree, to try to assess whether it has helped stimulate any sense of wonder. Their enthusiasm for accumulating knowledge of strange trees, processes of growth, or peculiar adaptations can serve as an index of the degree to which the topic has engaged their sense of wonder. Their sense of a balanced ecological ideal of good management of trees can indicate the degree to which they have developed an understanding of trees' role in the environment. Teachers' sensitivity to such dimensions of students' engagement with the topic can provide an imprecise but very real evaluation of how far they are being successful in stimulating students' imaginations, arboreally.

Note: Lest it be assumed that I have vast knowledge about trees to draw on, I should mention that all the information in this example comes from a single book review—Stephen Mills's (1990) review of John Perlin's *A Forest Journey: The Role of Wood in the Development of Civilization* (New York: Norton, 1990), and from the usual half hour with the encyclopedia. To really flesh out this unit one might actually read Perlin's book!

Chapter Three

A Tool Kit for Theoretic Thinking

Oh dear, another chunk of jargon up front. . . . What distinguishes this *theoretic thinking* from the kinds of thinking I have been talking about so far? And what set of cognitive tools is operating in it? Everyone has some sense of what theoretic thinking means. The trouble with using the term in a chapter title is that I run the danger of making into jargon something that has had a perfectly happy life in people's minds designating something perhaps not as specific as I want to use it for here.

An example might help introduce what I mean by the term. My wife and I were driving one of our sons to soccer when he was about fourteen. We were coming up to a federal election, and many of the lawns and windows we passed had sprouted posters in bright red, blue, yellow, and green encouraging us to vote for one or another candidate and party. In the election four years earlier, our children had been interested in how many signs were up for "our" candidate, who had the most signs and the biggest signs, which party was likely to win, and how anyone could vote for the villains who opposed our good guys. Putting his soccer boots on in the car, on this later occasion, our son asked whether we had to pay to have a sign on our lawn, and whether people with the really big signs had to pay more, or did the candidates pay us to put signs on our lawns. I told him that the candidates and their parties paid to have the signs made, or made them themselves, and people put them on their lawns freely to show their support. "But why would people vote for some party because of a sign on a lawn?"—he reasonably asked, adding, "If the parties and candidates represented particular social values and priorities, wouldn't people vote based on their principles, rather than be swayed by lawn signs?" We discussed this for a while, and his questions spread to the ways in which lawn signs were a part of the process of democratic elections.

My point is not just to show off what a clever bunch of kids we have (though . . .) but rather to indicate an example of a shift in thinking and in the set of cognitive tools being brought into play. And my purpose isn't to try to explain *why* this change occurs, typically in the mid-teens among students who have continued to develop their literate cognitive tools, but rather to describe some of its features in a way that illustrates how teachers might engage the *theoretic* imagination in learning. (An attempt at explaining *why* this change occurs can be found in Egan, 1997.)

So I'll begin as in preceding chapters with an advance organizer describing the new set of cognitive tools. I assume that this chapter will be of most interest to senior high school and college teachers, though some of these tools will have begun embryonic development in many younger students and could be used in earlier years where teachers think appropriate. Trying to compact these ideas into a table has been a challenge, and as I look at some of the definitions, they seem a bit clotted. But they do give some idea about these cognitive tools, and I will elaborate and clarify them below— I hope.

Cognitive Tools

Here are some of the main cognitive tools students will possess in greater or lesser degree as they develop theoretic thinking:

The sense of abstract reality	is a tool that enables us to make sense of the world in terms of ideas. The developing mind begins to construct an abstract world of general concepts that represent reality in a new way. It permits understanding of the processes by which

nature and society work and of our increasing control over these processes. It takes shape as part of the development of disembedded, rational, logically structured forms of thinking.

The sense of agency   is a tool that enables us to recognize ourselves as related to the world via complex causal chains and networks. This enables us to become more realistic in understanding how we can play roles in the real world, and understand ourselves as products of historical and social processes.

Grasp of general ideas and their anomalies   is a tool that enables us to perceive and construct abstract ideas about nature, society, history, and human psychology—and then recognize their inadequacy and rebuild them into more complex ideas.

The search for authority and truth   is a tool that helps assess the worth of general ideas, testing their validity so that meaning can be derived from them. This takes on a particular shape and importance with the development of abstract theoretic thinking, which seeks an objective, certain, privileged view of reality. Among the historical products of this cognitive tool at work have been dictionaries, encyclopedias, and textbooks—repositories of secured knowledge.

Meta-narrative understanding is a tool that orders facts or events into general ideas and allows us to form emotional associations with them. That is, we don't just organize facts into theories, we shape even our theories into more general meta-narratives that further shape our emotional commitments.

Here again, the above cognitive tools come into focus when we take the engagement of students' imaginations as a central concern. If engaging students' imaginations is held steadily to the fore as a condition of successful teaching, then these are the sort of categories that represent the kinds of things to which we should attend.

If we think of our task as not just teaching knowledge and skills, but as also engaging our students with the general ideas that underlie the knowledge and skills they are learning, we will be able to make our teaching more engaging to their imaginations, more meaningful to them, and more interesting for ourselves as well.

Also, the tools discussed in preceding chapters—stories, binary opposites, metaphors, mental images, extremes and limits, associating with heroes, the sense of wonder, and the rest—do not go away when theoretic abstractions develop. They remain available to be used.

The Sense of Abstract Reality

My son's discussion of election lawn signs illustrates how the everyday reality of visible things begins to generate another reality made up of general ideas. What happened during this conversation—and during other conversations and in subjects he was learning at school and seeing on TV—was the generation of new meaning to the idea of politics and to the idea of society and to the idea of democracy. In addition, these hugely abstract ideas were being connected one to another as well. In the past, no doubt he understood—in the sense of being able to give some adequate definition of—the words *politics, society,* and *democracy.* But the conversation in the car indicated that these words were taking on new and quite significantly different meanings.

No doubt he had used these words in conversations before, but they were now beginning to appear in discussions more frequently and prominently. They were no longer words he knew the meanings of; they had become, in some sense, "things" in their own right. *Society* was not now a rarely used and rather vague term; it used to refer vaguely to houses and families and neighborhoods and social services and the government, and so on. Now it was gathering precise meaning as an abstract composite of all those things.

Theoretic thinking is the development of this new world of abstract ideas and the growing ability to think in terms of these abstractions, and then connect the results of abstract thinking back to the concrete world. We can see it, and feel something of the difficulty of this kind of thinking, in those familiar word puzzles in math that ask, for example, "If a man took a train headed east from Albuquerque at 60 miles an hour and another man took a train traveling at 80 miles an hour from . . ." and invite the student to calculate where they would pass each other (see Gerofsky, 2004, for an interesting discussion of these word problems). What students would like to be able to do with such problems is stay in the real world and watch the actual trains—from about a mile up—and observe where they pass each other. But this is math class, and what the teacher wants the students to do is leave behind the world of the anonymous man on the train from Albuquerque and abstract the problem from the real-world situation and convert it into numbers and apply a formula and calculate where the two men would pass. The problem includes no invitation to wonder whether they are sad or happy, or tall or short, or are good at baseball, or fathers of sons who want to know why people would vote for a candidate because there are lots of lawn signs with her name on it. Instead it presents an invitation to enter the realm of abstract reality.

During the period when literacy drives the development of the cognitive tools discussed in Chapter Two, the student's engagement of reality is quite different from that which occurs with the development of abstract theoretic thinking. We might get some clearer sense of the difference by thinking of students' educational development as like exploring a landscape, or finding their way around that Italian hill town I generously, virtually, took you to in Chapter Two. Students use the tools they developed earlier to explore by trying to get a sense of the most extreme features of the environment, finding out its limits, looking in awe at the biggest buildings, locating the main square, and so on. But now, faced by the same task, they would set about drawing a map, an overview, an image of the relationships of all the pieces within the whole. That is, they will now always search for a general view.

In the imaginative classroom the language of the theoretical world will be commonly used, but the teacher will consistently support the students in understanding this language and using it themselves. The support can come by giving frequent examples of the particular elements from which the general words are derived. When, for example, the word *society* is used, the teacher will not assume that all students will have in place a robust theoretic sense of its meaning. So, on occasion, the teacher can elaborate a bit, reminding students how the term developed. I find that a dictionary of word origins can be invaluable for supporting the development of theoretic cognitive tools. So, in five minutes or less, the teacher can discover that the word comes from the Latin *socius*, which means a companion. Our society is made up of our companions, that is, people who share common purposes—actually, *companion* means literally people who share bread with us, from *cum* (with) and *panis* (bread). The word *society* began to be used more commonly in the nineteenth century, when society began to become more complex, and people increasingly felt they maybe didn't feel very companionable with many people in their shared society. The abstraction of the word suggests something of the difficulty people have now of being more precise about what everyone in a society shares in common.

Well, what I intended to show here is not some accurate etymology but rather the kind of talk that can draw students in the direction of theoretic thinking. Having begun talking about *society* like this, you can ask students for opinions about why the term became more common at the time when society became more complex and alienating for many. Then you might spend five minutes with the word *alienating*. But it might be useful to bear in mind that there is also a class to teach on some other topic!

Everything we teach will have theoretic dimensions, and teachers will be able to stimulate and develop students' imaginations by being alert to the various theoretic paths that lead to and from whatever is being taught. If we are teaching about light in physics, it will be helpful to alert students to the main theoretical disputes that have taken place and continue to take place about the nature of light, and the same goes for Shakespeare, or the geography of ocean floors, or calculus, or anything. The trick for the teacher is being aware of the extent of theoretical thinking the particular group of students can handle by themselves, and be ready to provide support to those less sure-footed in this rather heady realm.

The Sense of Agency

My son's lawn sign questions also hint at another shift that was going on in his thinking. Four years earlier, at the preceding election, he was interested in "sides" and in what our chances were of beating the main opponents, and so on. None of his earlier questions suggested that this was some process in which he had any part, except as an observer or through his parents. But in the car he is beginning to see that the lawn signs were just one part of a general process. His environment, that is, begins to shift from one of particular events and objects to one in which particular events and objects are parts of more general processes, which can only be understood by allowing words like *society, politics,* or *democracy* to become infused with new, important meaning.

As my son begins to see the world as one in which abstractly described processes are both common and important for understanding, he also begins to develop a sense of himself as having a role to play in these processes. His very "self," he begins to realize, is also a part of various processes. He is who he is—he increasingly understands—as a result of things that happened in the past; he is part of a historical process. He comes to realize: "I was born with a past" (MacIntyre, 1981, p. 205). With the development of the cognitive tool that allows clearer understanding of abstract processes comes the development of an understanding of oneself as having a role to play in those processes. As theoretic thinking becomes more elaborated, so too will students' sense of themselves as agents in social, historical, political, and familial processes.

In the imaginative classroom we will seek to encourage the development of this cognitive tool by encouraging students to take part in activities that will help stimulate their sense of agency. Most subjects in the curriculum can go beyond simple mastery of the material to offer opportunities for students to look outward to society in general and recognize that they can play roles of value or pleasure. Service activities are one common way to support this developing cognitive tool; students can help out at elections, interview old people they know or can be put in touch with, write letters to politicians on issues that have come up in their classes, or write letters to historical figures they have been learning about—Napoleon is as likely to read them as some politicians today! They can be encouraged to vote in online referenda on issues that interest them, and they can help out with some environmental preservation or reclamation project, involve themselves in church activities, or help a group of friends form a club or team of some kind.

Math examples that focus on important local issues, bringing statistical clarity where there has been only rhetoric, can lead to a letter to the newspaper. Geography examples can lead to a reclamation project. Historical studies that enlighten a current political issue can be written up and sent to participants in the issue. (I often think current proponents of voucher systems in education might benefit from a brief and clear account of the late-nineteenth-century "payment by results" schemes in England). Implications of physics or chemistry studies can be directed to outside groups for whom they have relevance. The purpose of these quick examples is not to engage students in some particular form of activism, or to select for the curriculum things that are especially relevant to current social conditions, but to show how the regular curriculum yields endless examples of new learning that students can use to stimulate and develop their sense of agency within the processes that surround them.

General Ideas and Their Anomalies

Theoretic thinking is accompanied by, or caused by, the development of a perspective on the world that begins with the general, so that events and objects are seen in terms of the process, system, or whole of which they are parts. Perhaps the easiest example of this is the students' understanding of history. During the earlier period, they saw history as a series of dramatic events and characters, styles of dress and modes of shelter, and so on. The students' interest was caught by the heroic character, the courageous rebellion, the wise ruler, the astonishing achievement, the exotic customs. Now these are no longer seen as more or less isolated characters and incidents. They are understood in terms of the complex process of history, as examples of a continuum of styles and customs, of a range of possible human behaviors within physical, psychological, and emotional constraints.

The meaning of historical events is now located in some general belief about the whole process, and the meaning of particular events is derived from that conception of the whole. The arrival of Columbus in North America is no longer seen simply as a heroic achievement full of good, or evil, consequences. It is seen rather as an element in large narratives of technological development, of national cohesiveness and royal or bourgeois investments, of patterns of disease and immunity, of the spread of plant species around the planet, of the character of European culture as exemplified in its contacts and conflicts with aboriginal Americans and the character of American cultures as exemplified in their contact and conflicts with Europeans, and in dozens of large meta-narratives that can be used to prescribe the meaning of the contact. By seeing the event in light of multiple meta-narratives, students will learn the complexity of the "truth" of the event, and Columbus's role in multiple narratives will further the process of sophistication of theoretic thinking.

Some students who develop theoretic thinking may conclude, for example, that the huge generalization that the world is going to hell in a handcart is true. They will accept without much qualification that stupid and greedy decisions are being made that will wreck our environment, run us out of fuel supplies, destroy our industries and cities, and so on. Alternatively, other students might conclude that the world is gradually getting better, that human beings do create crises for themselves but their energy and ingenuity always solve the problems, and that life is on an uneven but gradually upward curve toward a better future for all. We may call such people pessimists and optimists, though they all call themselves realistic. But their pessimism and optimism have been made into theories of history and society. There is no use simply confronting either of these positions with the opposite, as each will think the others are simply ignoring the important information that supports the right set of beliefs and is instead focused on superficial and largely irrelevant facts.

Pessimism and optimism become theories of history and society.

The route to developing theoretic thinking is in part a familiar old technique. We sometimes call it the dialectic—questioning and answering in defense of some hypothesis. Most commonly, for example, it might involve the optimist and the pessimist questioning and answering each other in an attempt to reach the truth. Of course, what such a method usually achieves is greater sophistication in methods of argument—not agreement about the truth.

Students who are inclined to believe that everything is going to hell in a handcart (a phrase that sounds better than the image it generates) can be helped to make their belief more complicated by being shown specific cases of obvious improvement in people's lives. One might point to surgical techniques that enable older people with arthritic joints to get around with greater ease and less pain. The pessimistic student will have no difficulty accepting that some things, like this, may be getting better, but will maintain that on the whole, things are getting worse. The example serves as an anomaly to the general belief. It is not a counterargument; it is not part of an argument for an optimistic view of current conditions and their general direction. It is just an anomaly to the general belief. Nonetheless, the belief must be reformulated, in however small a way, to take account of the exceptions to the general view.

One might then add other anomalies. One might point to the eradication of certain diseases. This might encourage the pessimistic student to modify the general belief a little more, or it might lead to the claim that eradicating diseases only makes overpopulation worse and will hasten the catastrophic effects of mass starvation. One might then add the anomaly to this position that more food per person is being produced now. And so on. The teacher might provide similar kinds of anomalies to the students who take the optimistic view.

In positing anomalies to any belief or general position, the aim is not to disprove the belief but simply to compel its holders to make their position more and more sophisticated. The fruit of this procedure is not Truth with a capital T, but an eventual recognition by the students that such general truths are not realizable. There are good grounds to think some things are getting better and that some are getting worse. Even if, during this century, we run out of breathable air and drinkable water, and perhaps blow up the planet, this won't prove the pessimists' current hypothesis true. It will mean that the grounds for their present predictions were well founded. But that is different from the general belief that they are true. What this more complex and sophisticated condition achieves is a reduction of general and unsustainable ideological and metaphysical beliefs about human nature, society, and history. And this condition of mind should allow us to focus more clearly on current problems and hopes behind which we can throw our efforts.

Why am I dragging you through this rather vague and general discussion? Well, I wanted to sketch a pedagogical method that is particularly useful for helping students develop theoretic thinking. Forming general ideas and then dealing with anomalies to those ideas is one of the main tools for furthering students' education once this process of building abstract worlds has begun. It's not the quantity of physics or history they learn that will make our students more educated, it is the degree of sophistication of the theoretic thinking they develop in the process of learning physics and history that is crucial, and the sophistication of the theoretic thinking they use to understand the physics and history. Indeed, and hardly coincidentally, to move through this process, the students will have to learn a great deal of physics and history and other subjects. The anomalies only work if they spur students on to discover new knowledge to defend their increasingly precariously held theories and general schemes.

Anomalies only work if they spur students on to discover new knowledge to defend their increasingly precariously held theories and general schemes.

The Search for Authority and Truth

A tool one can see constantly at work in theoretic thinking is the search for a bedrock for knowledge and beliefs. It isn't enough to accept some set of inherited beliefs. One needs to establish that they are True, and if they aren't, then one must find those that are. This search for security extends through all the theoretic thinker's life, even to quite trivial things. The sense that truth and meaning are to be located first in the general and abstract drives the theoretic thinker constantly, even if subconsciously sometimes, to look for the abstract source in which authority and truth can be located. If the abstract thinker loves singing, it will no longer be sufficient to simply prefer some singer over another—it will become needful to draw up criteria for goodness in singers, and compare singers in terms of these criteria. As theoretic thinking becomes more sophisticated, this becomes a tricky business. Callas may seem best according to some criteria, but Bartoli better according to others. Perhaps one should have different criteria and categories for contraltos and sopranos? Callas at some times in her career was better than others, and Bartoli is not so good with some composers, and . . . and. . . . For the fan of boxing, there will appear the drive to decide criteria that determine goodness of boxers. Was Ali the greatest, as he said, or Louis? But should we have different criteria for heavyweights than for lighter weights? But maybe the ultimate criterion would be who would win in a bout between the various boxers at their peak? But on some days, a lucky move or unexpected blow could change the whole course of a fight from the way it might have gone some other day, and . . . and. . . .

Trying to sort out preferences and beliefs leads constantly to reflection on the criteria that are appropriate, the sources of authority for beliefs. This transition is visible in all areas of life; from participating in social events to developing social theories, from participating in religious practices to developing a theology, from participating in everyday life as it passes to developing a theory of history, from participating in politics to developing an ideology, and so on. In each of these cases, and so many others, we see another side of the development of that abstract realm of ideas, and, within that abstract realm, attempts to sort out how to know securely, what to rely on, how to establish some basis for ideas. It's hard work, and most people don't do much of it unless supported by a community such as a school or college or university or reading and study groups consciously dedicated to developing abstract thinking. That community can also include certain kinds of journals, TV shows, lectures, discussions with particular people, and so on.

In the imaginative classroom what we see in these examples will be applied to all areas of the curriculum. If we want to engage the theoretic thinker's imagination in learning, we need to make sure that we present particular knowledge in a context that invites the student to see the knowledge in terms of some general and abstract idea. The more general and abstract the better initially. Historical facts can be presented within a context of huge historical processes—the kinds of meta-narratives addressed in one of the examples in the next (half!) chapter; students will be expected to learn about the impact of revolutions on the history of society.

Facts about particular animals can be presented in the context of theories about speciation; students will be expected to learn about the behavior of voles in the context of evolutionary theory and environmental ideas. What would happen if all the voles disappeared? What kind of environmental disaster would result? How about the disappearance of mosquitoes? How can we know whether the evolutionary accounts of mammal development are accurate? Facts about social groups can be presented in the context of sociological and anthropological ideas; students will be expected to learn about shopping statistics to support or challenge theories about human nature or in the context of cross-cultural comparisons. Has shopping replaced religion for some people? Are the economic benefits derived from consumption of certain goods that do little if anything for the lives of many consumers offset by spiritual desiccation and environmental degradation, or not? How could we reliably compare such things? What are the benefits to our patterns of shopping compared to the way people in oral cultures gathered what they needed and wanted?

Not great examples, perhaps, but the point is that the imagination at this stage will be more readily engaged if the particular is always seen in some more general context, and particularly if each new piece of knowledge can play a role in challenging or supporting some developing general idea or belief.

Meta-Narrative Understanding

Meta-narratives are overarching narratives; they are techniques for organizing facts, events, beliefs, ideas into general wholes that orient our emotions to the elements that make them up. Remember the discussion of stories in Chapter One? Meta-narratives share with the simplest story the shaping of emotion, but in this case the constituent parts of the meta-narrative that are organized into some new whole form the material of theoretic thinking. The meta-narrative might be concerned to orient moral or aesthetic or social or other emotions, so it provides a very general perspective.

So, for example, one might make some sense of the conflicts and language evident in the aftermath of the destruction of the World Trade Center twin towers on September 11, 2001, by viewing the event through the competing meta-narratives of Christian and Islamic traditions. In the West, this event is fitted into a meta-narrative in which it can be described only as the evil act of terrorists, in response to which a "war on terrorism" is justified. The connection of this meta-narrative with a long, largely Christian tradition of Western expansion and liberalization made it easy for the president of the United States, George W. Bush, to talk about the response of American forces as a "crusade." In a militant Islamic meta-narrative, the oppressive Western "devils" were being struck by heroic soldiers of God who sacrificed their lives rather than accept continual oppression and the suppression of their way of life. The invasive pressure of Western capitalism and its associated ideologies is seen as simply a continuation by other means of the violent and destructive crusades of earlier centuries. Other forms of this meta-narrative appear in conflicts between globalism and multiculturalism, sustainability and growth, and so on. A few decades ago, Marxist and Capitalist meta-narratives might have proved more apposite as examples.

You can see, in the rather crude description of the competing meta-narratives that make different sense of the World Trade Center conflagration, how a meta-narrative is not just a logical structuring device but is primarily responsible for orienting emotion. No one is disputing the central facts and events; it's their meaning that is shaped by the meta-narrative an individual is using. And as our emotions are commonly caught up in establishing the meaning of events and facts, meta-narratives will play an important role in educational development. We may spend much of our adult lives trying to shake off crude meta-narratives that mislead our minds, but the educational answer is not to ignore or suppress the use of this tool because it might mislead us but rather to use it sensibly, understanding clearly how it can help achieve particular important ends. (Just as no one argues for the destruction of hammers because they are not useful for sawing and can help smash things, so it would be silly to argue for the avoidance of meta-narratives because they can have bad consequences if misused. Any tool, workbench or cognitive, can be misused. The educational virtue is to understand the available tools and to understand and teach how each may be best used.)

A final characteristic of this cognitive tool of theoretic thinking also raises another point of wariness about its use; that is, meta-narratives can be exciting. When we first develop the control of varied material by fitting it into some meta-narrative, it gives us a new kind of understanding and sense of power over the material. We see its meaning— in a new and powerful way. For some people, the development of meta-narratives grows relatively slowly, and this sense of exciting intellectual power is muted. But for others it comes quickly and can be intoxicating. It can strike with great force, suggesting to such individuals that at last they finally *see*. It is as though they come to grasp the truth behind appearances, the abstract reality that gives meaning to the concrete elements of the everyday world.

The pedagogical importance and uses of this excitement can easily be underestimated—when they are noticed at all!—and can easily be abused. So, again, dangers come with this potent intellectual tool. But there is more educational (and perhaps other) danger in not noticing it. Only think what a sensitive educator might have done to make more sophisticated and then displace the meta-narratives of people like Hitler or Stalin. (I recognize that their problems and policies were not simply a result of inadequate teaching while they were in school! But the power of a good teacher can achieve the miraculous, daily.) Too frequently teachers in the higher grades and at college level focus on the curriculum exclusively and do not see the students' developing cognitive tools in the curriculum material. Consequently, they do not recognize how their subject can generate intellectual excitement in students.

This leads to two problems: first, such teachers simply do nothing to further the most important aspect of their students' intellectual development, and, second, whatever development of meta-narratives does occur is allowed to occur randomly and uncontrolled, with no systematic use of anomalies to generate greater sophistication. In the first case, learning will become drudgery and remain largely inert for students, failing to engage their imaginations. In the second case, the students may develop crude and simplistic ideologies, metaphysical schemes, and so on—the Hitler/Stalin problem.

In the imaginative classroom an array of the most powerful meta-narratives generated in our history will be frequently called-upon tools. The aim of the educational process is recognition that meta-narratives are always inadequate, always hopelessly less rich and complex than the reality they try to represent. In science, Thomas Kuhn's hugely successful meta-narrative about scientific revolutions should be discussed at least once or twice in science classes. History studies have to keep grappling with whether things are getting better or worse, in various of the more or less sophisticated versions of these ideas. The constant raising of general theories also, at this level, serves a purpose not unlike that of raising the sense of mystery in younger students. Each works to develop cognitive tools of considerable power, enabling students to make better sense of their lives and world.

The aim of the educational process is recognition
that meta-narratives are always inadequate,
always hopelessly less rich and complex than
the reality they try to represent.

Conclusion

The educational tool kit doesn't stop with theoretic thinking, but the structure of this book makes it preferable to avoid discussion of ways to draw the student forward to the next set of cognitive tools. Those tools reveal ways in which theoretic thinking, helpful as it is, is inadequate to the reality it is supposed to represent or explain. (See Egan 1997, Chapter 5 for a sense of what this further tool kit contains.)

Over and above the lack of an embryonic-tools section, I recognize that this chapter may seem to have less variety than its predecessors. Indeed, some of the discussion might seem as though it could fit into another section without too much difficulty. And there is some truth to that. Theoretic thinking is very various in practice but, not inappropriately, its main characteristic is the same in whatever area it is being used. The drive for the general, the abstract, the secure basis for theories, the bedrock of belief, the source of authority, the truth—all lead to the elaboration of the theoretic world, the world of ideas.

And this kind of theoretic thinking might seem to be confusing rather than useful to the student. It does have difficult features; it is hard work to develop and sustain—so hard, indeed, that no one can manage it alone. Students—like all of us—need a theoretic community to keep it going. If its main purpose is the generation of an abstract world of ideas, ideas that are difficult to keep clear and straight, and we are to spend a fair amount of effort generating anomalies to anything the students come to believe so that we can get them over it, then what's its value? Well, it is a kind of thinking that gives students great power and control over the stuff they think with; it enhances thinking ability enormously, enabling them to put the diversity of what they have learned into a new kind of order. It also generates flexibility, encourages them to search out patterns, look for essences, and, most typically, construct theories. This set of tools gives its holders more pragmatic control over the world.

One point may be worth emphasizing here, and that concerns the degrees of theoretic thinking that a person can develop. Clearly we see people who hold to some theory or theology or ideology that is very rigid and who seem to use this idea as a means of holding off other ideas and of avoiding thinking. Sometimes we see such forms of thinking as very crude and their holders as largely ignorant even of knowledge that is relevant to their beliefs. I think one could describe these as people who may have experienced a brief burst of theoretic thinking but have cut it off from development. They do not experience the increasing sophistication and flexibility that come from acknowledging anomalies to their theories or beliefs and making their beliefs or theories more sophisticated to take account of the anomalies. That process—building knowledge to support the theory or belief and being challenged and responding by seeking further supporting knowledge—simply doesn't get under way.

Which also raises a final point for this chapter—the crucial role that expanding knowledge plays in driving the development of the abstract world of ideas. Ideas become rich and flexible and strong as they are supported and challenged by the constant growth of knowledge. A central feature of imaginative education that I have touched on here and there, but is worth emphasizing again and again, is that for the imagination to develop adequately and to work effectively the student needs to know a lot. Ignorance is not a condition that favors the development of imagination.

Ideas become rich and flexible and strong as they are supported and challenged by the constant growth of knowledge.

Ignorance is not a condition that favors the development of imagination.

Chapter Three and a Half

Examples in Everyday Classrooms

The framework that follows is designed for teaching students who are typically at the higher grades of high school or at colleges and universities. Mostly, teachers at these levels tend not to spend much time reflecting on teaching methodology. Which, I suppose, means I am writing this chapter primarily for people who are not usually inclined to read things like this. They might benefit by doing so, however; my hope is that their friends who teach younger students—and their professors of education and workshop leaders—will draw their attention to this framework.

There is an assumption—which has some obvious truth to it—that the logic of the subject matter is the crucial thing to sort out to be able to teach effectively at these levels. That is, for chemistry in grade eleven or twelve or beyond, most teachers focus their attention on making the topic clear, getting the requisite knowledge into the best order in the sequence of instruction, and organizing teaching according to the logic of the subject.

And this approach generally works quite well—in good measure because by this time in their schooling students have shuffled into specializing in those areas they learn best. So Grade 12 or college-level chemistry students are in some degree self-selected for learning

---

Note: I faced something of a problem writing examples of math and science units at this level. I just didn't know about any topic in enough detail to be able to do the job easily. So I turned to David Egan—the son you met in Chapter Three, tying his bootlaces in the car on the way to soccer during an election campaign—to provide the requisite knowledge. He has kindly written Example Two (Calculus) and Example Four (Simple Harmonic Motion) for this chapter, and in the process illustrates how the sections of the framework can be modified to suit the material.

this way—they are good at working with logically organized knowledge, good at remembering facts, and so on. The possible problem with this is that because the dominant form of teaching during these years tends to reflect the logic of the subject rather than the cognitive tools the students will have developed, we tend to select students for the sciences and mathematics who are good at what has been called "disembedded" learning. They are the students who can learn anything because they have a facility for learning, even if what they are learning doesn't engage their imaginations or emotions at all. For other students, if knowledge fails to engage their imaginations and emotions, they develop a distaste for it, and so turn away from subjects taught in such a manner as not to engage them.

The purpose of the approach to teaching being promoted in this book and series, however, is to engage all students' imaginations in whatever is to be learned, and consequently to ensure that it is meaningful and emotionally important. One result of this approach, I think, is that it will improve students' engagement with (and competence in) the sciences and mathematics and will also considerably widen the range of students who are attracted to these important areas of human inquiry.

Well, I just needed to get that off my chest. And of course this chapter is not going to limit itself to math and science; it's just that those areas of study best exemplify the problem of designing teaching that suits only a small subset of students, which is also a problem for other areas of study, I think, but more visible in the sciences and in math.

Another point I'd like to make before getting on with the heavy lifting of this chapter concerns the likelihood, given our present forms of education, that many students in the final grades of high school and at college and university will still be most easily engaged by teaching that uses the cognitive tools outlined in Chapter Two. That is, not all students develop all (or even most) of the cognitive tools described in Chapter Three. This kind of abstract theoretic discourse just isn't generally well developed by current forms of schooling. And life outside school, particularly in the various public media that currently saturate the landscape, sees hardly any support for it. However, if we develop the sequence of cognitive tools described in the preceding chapters then I think we might reasonably expect a much higher proportion of students to develop this kind of theoretic understanding in the future.

The final preliminary point is just a reminder that the cognitive tools described in earlier chapters don't simply go away with the development of this new set. They are all still there to be used. The final example in this chapter indicates how we can relatively easily incorporate many of the cognitive tools discussed earlier in designing a lesson or unit at this level.

Third Planning Framework: Full-Blown

So here is a framework that incorporates most of the cognitive tools discussed in the previous chapter. In this case I won't bother with a simplified version but will go straight to the fully developed and supportive version.

Third Planning Framework

1. *Identifying powerful underlying ideas:* What underlying ideas or theories seem best able to organize the topic into some coherent whole? What are the most powerful, clear, and relevant theories, ideologies, metaphysical schemes, or meta-narratives?
2. *Organizing the content into a theoretic structure:*
   2.1. Initial access: How can the underlying theory or idea be made vivid? What content best exposes it and shows its power to organize the topic?
   2.2. Organizing the body of the lesson or unit: What meta-narrative provides a clear overall structure to the lesson or unit?
3. *Introducing anomalies to the theory:* What content is anomalous to the general idea or theory? How can we begin with minor anomalies and gradually and sensitively challenge the students'

general theory so that they make the theory increasingly sophisticated?

4. *Presenting alternative general theories:* What alternative general theories can organize the topic? What alternative meta-narrative can organize the topic? Which can best be used to help students see something about the nature and limitations of their theories and meta-narratives?

5. *Encouraging development of the students' sense of agency:* What features of the knowledge will best allow us to encourage the students' developing sense of agency?

6. *Conclusion:* How can we ensure that the student's theories or general ideas are not destroyed but are recognized as having a different status from the facts they are based on? How can we ensure that the decay of belief in the Truth of theories or general ideas does not lead to disillusion and alienation?

7. *Evaluation:* How can we know whether the content has been learned and understood, whether students have developed a theory or general idea, elaborated it, and attained some sense of its limitations?

1. *Identifying Powerful Underlying Ideas.* *What underlying ideas or theories seem best able to organize the topic into some coherent whole? What are the most powerful, clear, and relevant theories, ideologies, metaphysical schemes, or meta-narratives?*

These theories may be political, scientific, economic, social, literary, philosophical, or any other kind that claim to explain the material to be learned. The core task in teaching through this framework is to clarify and make conscious those schemes, ideas, or theories (which may or may not have been evident to students before) and to enable students to recognize them as undergirding the area they are learning about, and to begin to question them. One way that might help the teacher to focus on the powerful underlying ideas is to consider the main controversies surrounding the topic—what do people generally argue about?

Things to List:

- The most powerful underlying idea or theory in this topic:
- An alternative:

2. Organizing the Content into a Theoretic Structure. This is a two-step process:

2.1. Initial Access. How can the underlying theory or idea be made vivid? What content best exposes it and shows its power to organize the topic?

This section involves planning what will form the basis of the first teaching act of the unit or lesson. Having identified the most powerful underlying theory or idea, the teacher's next job is to reflect on the topic as a whole and locate some aspect of it in which the theory or idea is most vividly clear. Usually this will be something that is central and profound about the topic. Often the selection will require a look at the *context* of the topic in the area of knowledge of which it is a part. So if you're looking at, say, the French Revolution in history, you might begin by reflecting on the nature of revolutions, or on differences and similarities among social, political, religious, cultural, economic, or other kinds of revolution. This will encourage students to develop theories about revolutions in general, which will generate an abstract, theoretic context for the particular study of the French Revolution.

Alternatively, you could focus on the particulars of the French Revolution itself, asking the students to reflect on whether it was a tragic event in European history, with some possibly good effects, or whether it was a liberating and progressive event in European history, with some regrettable excesses. Alternatively, you could locate a very powerful representation, written or visual, that vividly exposes the theory or idea that serves as an organizer of the content. You could read from Dickens's description of Madame Defarge knitting as the guillotine sliced aristocratic heads into the basket in front of her, for example, and reflect on the Revolution from her perspective. This is, as with the previous frameworks, often the most difficult but most crucial part of applying the framework.

Things to List:

• Content that exposes the scheme or theory most vividly:

2.2. Organizing the Body of the Lesson or Unit. What meta-narrative provides a clear overall structure to the lesson or unit?

Here the idea is to take the powerful general idea or theory just identified and use it to shape the structure of the lesson or unit of study into a coherent whole. Continuing the French Revolution example, you might select as most useful for your purposes the theory that the Revolution was a catastrophic event in European history, because it ruptured the traditional foundations of society and gave birth to the Terror and to dictatorship and hugely destructive wars. Having chosen this theory, you can build a meta-narrative account of the whole Revolution that selects facts and events to highlight this particular view and build it as the Truth about the Revolution. In other subjects, such as the sciences, for example, such a heavily loaded ideological position will not be usual, but there are equivalents in all areas of knowledge. Remember, putting the content into a (meta-) narrative form helps to engage students' emotions. That is, if the selected meta-narrative seems not to capture any idea that stimulates the students or the teacher, then the teacher needs to delve deeper, or delve elsewhere in the topic.

Things to List:

• Content that will present a strong meta-narrative of the topic:

---

3. *Introducing Anomalies to the Theory.* *What content is anomalous to the general idea or theory? How can we begin with minor anomalies and gradually and sensitively challenge the students' general theory so that they make the theory increasingly sophisticated?*

General ideas or theories attempt to provide a total explanation of the topic, but they can never do so. The teacher needs to focus attention on particular facts or events that present a challenge to the claim of the idea or theory to explain the Truth about the topic. What does the theory explain well and what does it fail to explain adequately? In the case of the French Revolution, the teacher will focus attention on those aspects of the topic that are clearly anomalous to the meta-narrative created so far. So the teacher will ask the students to look at the abuses of the old regime and at the many failed attempts to reform them. Then students' attention might be focused on the Napoleonic legal reforms, the removal of penalties against Jews, and other reforms that ushered in more liberal government and greater freedom for much of the population. The aim, remember, is not to persuade the students to switch from one meta-narrative to another but rather to change their understanding of the *status* of meta-narratives.

Things to List:

- Main anomalies to the meta-narrative:

---

4. *Presenting Alternative General Theories.* *What alternative general theories can organize the topic? What alternative meta-narrative can organize the topic? Which can best be used to help students see something about the nature and limitations of their theories and meta-narratives?*

Various theories can always be used to explain the same phenomena. Help students compare their coherence and explanatory power. In some curriculum areas this will be easier than others, but it is possible in all areas of knowledge. That is, while it may be relatively easy to shift from looking at the last years of the Chinese empire from the perspective of a Western liberal to that of an arch-conservative Mandarin to that of a Marxist enemy of the old regime and relatively difficult to come up with alternative perspectives for the theory of gravitation, analogous alternative views do exist about all meta-narratives.

> *Things to List:*
>
> • Alternative theories or meta-narratives that will be used:

5. Encouraging Development of the Students' Sense of Agency. *What features of the knowledge will best allow us to encourage the students' developing sense of agency?*

Teaching at this level is not only about ensuring the mastery of knowledge in various areas, it is concerned with ensuring that what is being learned is seen by the students as tying them to the knowledge by causal networks. Some part of the unit should focus on what the students can do in relation to the topic. Although learning about acid rain or other science topics may seem straightforwardly to lead to thinking about what actions out in the world that the new knowledge empowers one to take, it might seem unlikely that learning about history could yield the same sense of agency. But in any area of knowledge, the meta-narrative used will have public implications—knowledge of the French Revolution might encourage radical, conservative, or liberal ideas that can become a part of the student's power to articulate and take part in social and political plans of action.

> *Things to List:*
>
> • Areas in which students' sense of agency can be engaged and encouraged:

6. Conclusion. *How can we ensure that the students' theories or general ideas are not destroyed but are recognized as having a different sta-*

tus from the facts they are based on? How can we ensure that the decay of belief in the Truth of theories or general ideas does not lead to disillusion and alienation?

In units and lessons at this level, teachers should constantly take a direction that shows students that the theories and general ideas they develop and use in learning are not themselves like the facts and events that constitute the foundation of their study. In the earlier period, when students are developing theoretic thinking, it is best to downplay a little the challenges to their theories, ideas, ideologies, metaphysical schemes, and meta-narratives. With students who have already moved some way in the fluency with which they use theoretic thinking, teachers can safely work harder at providing anomalies and alternatives. In concluding any unit or lesson, however, students should at least receive strong hints about the difference between the theory that engages their emotions and the facts that support it, or support it in part, or fail to support it convincingly. Teachers will need to be sensitive to the state of students' theories and encourage their development while also showing their inadequacy as claims to Truth.

Things to List:

- Concluding activity designed both to support and show problems with students' theories, ideas, meta-narratives, and ideologies:

---

7. Evaluation. *How can we know whether the content has been learned and understood, whether students have developed a theory or general idea, elaborated it, and attained some sense of its limitations?*

The goal here is evidence that students have learned the content that has made up the lesson or unit of study. This can be attained by use of any of a variety of traditional techniques. At the same time, the teacher also needs evidence about how adequately students have developed some theory or general idea and used it in organizing the content they have learned. This could be evaluated in part by examining students' writing or oral discussions to see whether the theoretic language appropriate to the topic is deployed flexibly and correctly. One would also be able to judge to what degree students successfully generated order in the content by application of a general scheme to it. One could examine their written work also for evidence of increasing elaboration of their theories or general ideas in light of anomalies. Either casual cynicism about or committed devotion to the Truth of some scheme would indicate failures of teaching and learning, though unqualified commitment during the early period should not be a cause of much worry.

A general evaluation of how readily and fluently students use abstract ideas, and how committed they are to their use as a means of gaining a flexible understanding of the world, can be relatively easily read from their work and discussions—though it is difficult to be precise in scoring such readings. It would be useful perhaps to have rather gross categories in a continuum, from "Easy and Flexible" to "Adequate" to "Inadequate," available for teachers to score in evaluating students' performance. In part, such scales would be useful in sensitizing teachers to this dimension of students' performance.

Things to List:

- Forms of evaluation that will give adequate evidence that the students have learned and understood the content and also have developed and used some theory or abstract idea:

Example One: Revolutions

Earlier, introducing the French Revolution as an example, I mentioned that one could teach about revolutions in general, and that that could provide a topic that engages the imaginations of students and helps them use and develop their theoretic thinking. So let's run it through the framework—so to speak—and see whether a teachable unit emerges.

1. Identifying Powerful Underlying Ideas. *What underlying ideas or theories seem best able to organize the topic into some coherent whole? What are the most powerful, clear, and relevant theories, ideologies, metaphysical schemes, or meta-narratives?*

The most powerful underlying idea or theory in this topic: In most human activities things carry on according to a set of rules and conventions, but at irregular intervals someone who promises to make things better initiates radical change. This happens in history, religion, science, and every area of sustained activity we can see. Is revolution a law of human affairs?

An alternative: Is there a pattern to revolutions?

2. Organizing the Content into a Theoretic Structure. This is a two-step process:

2.1. Initial Access. How can the underlying theory or idea be made vivid? What content best exposes it and shows its power to organize the topic?

Content that exposes the scheme or theory most vividly: We can begin by examining in general terms political history and the series of prominent revolutions students may know about. Then we can look at the history of religion and see how normal conventional practices are disrupted at regular intervals, creating schisms or breaking off as new religions, which those who adhere to the old orthodoxy label heresies. Then we can look at science and see how "normal science" is interrupted by revolutionary theories that disrupt the pattern. We can then consider the Industrial and Technological Revolutions and their dramatic changes in forms of manufacturing. We can then ask the students to describe other forms of human activity, and ask them if they see a similar pattern in forms of music, drama, entertainment, sport, and so on?

2.2. Organizing the Body of the Lesson or Unit. What meta-narrative provides a clear overall structure to the lesson or unit?

Content that will present a strong meta-narrative of the topic: For this unit we could take an example of a revolution in the main spheres of human activity and examine it in some detail. Our alternative underlying theory might be brought into play here, in that we will invite students to see whether they can find a pattern in the revolutions they are to study.

We can start by reexamining the French Revolution, which most students will have studied in their history program. In this case we will direct students to focus on finding what caused the sudden change, why it should have happened then, and, in following its progress, what events were crucial in making it "revolutionary." What was the main dynamic of the Revolution?

We will begin to shape a theory of the Revolution, which will be stimulated further by asking students to compare the French Revolution with other revolutions. Different theories will begin to emerge as students identify different dynamics at work. The students can be asked to try to decide what is the essence of a revolution— what elements must be necessary for some change to be considered revolutionary?

We can leave the political and social revolution behind before reaching any firm conclusions, suggesting to the students that our understanding of revolution will be clarified if we take a different kind of revolution. We might look at the birth of Christianity, or Islam, or Confucianism. Let us, for the sake of this example, take Confucianism. We will ask students to study what we know of China prior to the birth of Confucius's ideas. What was it about his message at that time that resonated so strongly with many people? Why should suggesting that social harmony, supported by rulers' restraint and modesty and subjects' obedience and respect, be so powerful and revolutionary a message? Contrary to most people's belief, Confucius argued that, while harmony and respect were socially important, power should be gained by education and cultivating one's virtues, and that the virtuous person would be critical of rulers when appropriate. We can look closely at the dynamics that enabled Confucianism to grow and expand across China. How is the dynamic of Confucianism's revolution like and unlike that of the French Revolution?

We can at this point revisit the discussions about the nature of revolution. As they become more refined, and perhaps as disagreements become clearer, we can turn to a scientific revolution, such as that resulting from Einstein's theories of relativity. Why did they appear so revolutionary? What was the state of science before Einstein's work, and what was it about his theories that changed many physicists' views of the world and how they could study it?

We can look in detail at the changes that occurred and at the broad range of new ways of conceiving the subatomic and cosmic views of matter that resulted. We can consider how far the theories' association with such technological products as the atomic bomb led to Einstein's becoming an iconic figure of "the scientist," and how far that is responsible for his work's being considered revolutionary. We can then revisit our discussions about the nature of revolution with this further example, and we can bring our new ideas to bear on it.

At this point we can begin to study the Industrial Revolution, again focusing on causes, the actual changes, the technologies' effects on people's lives. The students' developing theories of revolution will begin to direct their search for particular kinds of causes, facts, events, and effects.

Depending on the time available, we could similarly explore other revolutions, constantly coming back to the question about the nature of revolution, constantly refining students' theories.

3. *Introducing Anomalies to the Theory.* *What content is anomalous to the general idea or theory? How can we begin with minor anomalies and gradually and sensitively challenge the students' general theory so that they make the theory increasingly sophisticated?*

To challenge the claim of the idea or theory to explain the Truth about the topic, look at what the theory explains well and what it fails to explain adequately. As noted earlier, the aim here is not to persuade the students to switch from one meta-narrative to another, but rather to change their understanding of the status of meta-narratives.

Main anomalies to the meta-narrative: We can begin by drawing to students' attention things that didn't change at all during each revolution. In reflecting on the French Revolution, ask them to find out what they can about the lives of peasants in France, particularly in the more remote regions. Did they even know there was a revolution going on? How many noble families are to be found after the Revolution with their fortunes intact?

What effects did the Industrial Revolution have on peasants' lives? Did it have significant impact on housing? If it is seen as a benefit to people in general, what effects did it have on those it attracted from the countryside into towns? If it is seen as a catastrophe, what are the statistics for child mortality and other diseases before and after?

In reflecting on the Industrial Revolution, some students may have formed the idea that the Revolution reflected a new industrial class coming to power. If so, they could be asked to trace the number of old landowning upper-class members who invested heavily in the new industries. Ask students to discover how much of the capital that financed the Industrial Revolution came from the slave trade and how far this might affect their theory about its causes.

We can continue to pose such anomalies to the students' theories about each of the revolutions they study, and they can be encouraged to pose anomalies to one another's theories. The aim of such anomalies is not to disprove the theory but to encourage the students to search for further knowledge that will both respond to the anomaly and support their theory.

4. Presenting Alternative General Theories. *What alternative general theories can organize the topic? What alternative meta-narrative can organize the topic? Which can best be used to help students see something about the nature and limitations of their theories and meta-narratives?*

Alternative theories or meta-narratives: We can explore two alternative general ideas—that revolutions are simply accelerated forms of the normal changes that go on all the time in all areas, or that they are qualitatively different shifts in experience, understanding, social life, and so on. We can ask the students to reconsider each of the revolutions they have seen in light of both of these meta-narratives. We might, first, look for signs prior to each revolution that things were moving in that general direction anyway, and focus on the facts and events that suggest that for many people what we call the revolution would have not appeared as dramatic as we assume in retrospect. Then we might ask the students to adopt the alternative general idea and look at the revolutions again as creating qualitative shifts, if not immediately, then over a relatively short period of time. The changes were not simply accelerations of the normal but led to dramatic and unpredictable events, kinds of understanding, modes of experience, and so on.

5. Encouraging Development of the Students' Sense of Agency. *What features of the knowledge will best allow us to encourage the students' developing sense of agency?*

Areas in which students' sense of agency can be engaged and encouraged: By drawing attention to the role of individuals in each of our revolutions, we can encourage students to see that there was nothing inevitable about their actions or the effects of their actions: that dramatic changes are often brought about by people in circumstances that are not special. That is, a study of revolutions can help students feel that they too can have major effects if they apply themselves in some specific way.

The teacher can take opportunities to draw students into thinking about what they would or could have done in the circumstances of each revolution.

6. Conclusion. *How can we ensure that the students' theories or general ideas are not destroyed but are recognized as having a different status from the facts they are based on? How can we ensure that the decay of belief in the Truth of theories or general ideas does not lead to disillusion and alienation?*

Concluding activity: The class could engage in a formal debate between those who view revolution as qualitative change and those who view it as accelerated normal change—business as usual, only faster. The students would use all the revolutions they have studied as material in making their arguments. The formal nature of a debate should provide adequate protection against alienation through disillusionment, and the support of those on their "team" will likely provide further defense against such an outcome.

In addition to the debate, the students might be encouraged to produce large murals illustrating the various kinds of revolution. Representing their knowledge in this different form can be helpful in crystallizing what is essential to their theory and what peripheral. If the murals are done in groups, the inevitable debates about how the revolution is to be represented can help students recognize that the overall pictures are not fixed in the same way as the facts or events that will be presented in various forms in all the representations of the revolutions.

7. Evaluation. *How can we know whether the content has been learned and understood, whether students have developed a theory or general idea, elaborated it, and attained some sense of its limitations?*

Forms of evaluation: Standard forms of evaluation can assess whether students have learned about the various kinds of revolutions, have understood their different forms, and can describe the salient characteristics of each revolution they have studied. For evidence that students have been able to form some defensible theory about the nature of revolution, we can assess the discussions in class (rating the coherence and explanatory power of students' theories on Likert scales) and also assign an essay that asks students to articulate their own theory about the nature of revolution.

A useful book to support this unit is Crane Brinton's *Anatomy of Revolution* (New York: Norton, 1938). There are no doubt other similar resources written more recently.

Example Two: Calculus (Ages Sixteen to Twenty)

In our changing world, calculus is the mathematical tool that formalizes change and expresses it in terms that make clear sense. In theory, any process of change, from the acceleration of a sprinter to the falling of autumn leaves, can be expressed as a mathematical function. Differential calculus provides the initial set of tools by which we can analyze these functions and develop a sense for the inner workings of processes of change. This two-to-three-week unit introduces students to the tools and methods of the differential calculus.

Calculus is a Latin word meaning *pebble* or *stone* (as it is still used in medicine and dentistry), and indicates that pebbles (prehistorically and later) were used to "calculate"—that is, to form conclusions about quantities.

1. Identifying Powerful Underlying Ideas. *What underlying ideas or theories seem best able to organize the topic into some coherent whole? What are the most powerful, clear, and relevant theories, ideologies, metaphysical schemes, or meta-narratives?*

The most powerful underlying idea or theory in this topic: Differential calculus was the first mathematical tool invented to measure change itself. Until the invention of the calculus in the late seventeenth century, mathematicians had been able to model only static states of affairs, or at best variable rates represented by functions. Calculus is the first tool to take change itself as an object of study, giving change a central place in our understanding of the universe.

An alternative: Calculus is shorthand for "infinitesimal calculus," because it deals with infinitesimal line segments, which have an infinitely small but non-zero length. How can we make sense of the infinitesimal, and how does this struggle clarify for us the concepts of infinity, continuity, and limit?

2. Organizing the Content into a Theoretic Structure. This is a two-step process:

2.1. Initial Access. How can the underlying theory or idea be made vivid? What content best exposes it and shows its power to organize the topic?

Content that exposes the scheme or theory most vividly: We can begin by asking what *change* in general is and how we register change in its different manifestations. What do getting dressed, melting snow, and revising our preconceptions about a person have in common that we can refer to all three of them in terms of a change taking place? A change involves a final state that is different from an initial state, yes, but what sorts of things might we be able to say of this progression from one state to another that might help us to understand it better? How long did it take? How different is the final state from the initial state, and in what way? What unit of measurement, if any, can we use to indicate the change? How might we observe or measure the change? What value is there in measuring change, and what difficulties are there?

One powerful conceptual tool for measuring change that students should already have is the polynomial function. Though a function might not seem the most obvious way of analyzing the process of changing clothes or changing minds, it can be instructive to examine how these processes can, at least in some sense, be expressed as polynomial functions. The class might enjoy the challenge of finding a way to graph, for example, a person's state of undress as a function of time.

2.2. Organizing the Body of the Lesson or Unit. What meta-narrative provides a clear overall structure to the lesson or unit?

Content that will present a strong meta-narrative of the topic: We can appreciate the power of calculus by understanding the revolutionary impact it had on the science of its day, and how it was in many ways the centerpiece in a more general revolution in human beings' understanding of the cosmos and their place in it. The infinitesimal calculus was developed by Newton and Leibniz (the conflicting claims to priority by these two figures, and the ensuing controversy, might also make an interesting topic of discussion) as a means of expressing change in mathematical terms. For the first time, scientists could study change in a rigorous and formalized manner, facilitating a whole new view of the universe as dynamic and changing rather than as static and fixed.

We can begin by looking at the medieval conception of the earth as fixed at the center of an ordered and harmonious cosmos.

We might consider Aristotle's assumption about inertia, taken for granted for many centuries, that everything will come to rest unless some force is constantly and actively keeping it in motion. That is, Aristotle and his medieval successors saw rest as the natural state of things. We can also look at the various ways in which this conception of a universe at rest was tied to the sociopolitical arrangements of the medieval world. For example, we could show how this conception of a fixed cosmos reflects the fixed social hierarchy of the day, placing kings at the top of a Great Chain of Being that allowed for little social mobility.

To better appreciate the historical place of the invention of calculus, we can consider the general change in the West's understanding of the world that came about during the Renaissance, setting off the development of the printing press, the discovery of the Americas, the Protestant Reformation, and so on. These developments set off in turn a series of new developments in the sciences, from Copernicus to Galileo to Kepler to Newton. The world ceased to be a fixed entity at the center of a universe whose natural tendency was toward rest, and came to be seen as one moving element in a dynamic and ever-changing cosmos. To make sense of this new cosmos, it was important to develop tools that could measure and quantify its nature. Enter calculus as the knight in shining armor to make sense of our dynamic universe.

3. Developing the Tools to Analyze the Theoretic Structure. *What mathematical or scientific tools will help us analyze the phenomena touched upon in the general idea or theory? How can we develop and explore these tools in a way that underlines their pertinence to the general idea or theory?*

Major tools and their pertinence: Students should already be familiar with polynomial functions and should know how to graph a curve and how to measure the slope of a line. They should also be familiar with sequences and series, and their attendant limits. Differential calculus is simply a matter of combining these familiar elements in new ways. Students will need to learn how to identify, measure, and express the limits of a function, recognize and plot tangents to curves that show the slope of a curve at a given point, and then to generalize these concepts of limit and slope to calculate the derivative of a polynomial function. Once students have learned the central concept of computing a derivative, the rest of the material consists simply of elaborations on this central concept. The power rule, the sum rule, the product rule, and the chain rule, as well as formulas for the derivatives of trigonometric functions and other tricky functions, all build on this central concept of the derivative.

While teaching these mathematical tools, it is worth constantly bearing in mind, and reminding the students, of the role these tools play in the larger narrative of developing a generalized means of analyzing change. We are trying to make the inner workings of change evident and clear to view. For instance, by drawing a line that is tangent to a curve, we are showing plainly just what the slope of the curve is at that infinitesimal point where curve and tangent meet. We are turning the elusive fluidity of a curve into a simple straight line. We are finding ways to make complicated things simpler.

4. Taking Account of the Limitations of the Theoretic Structure.
What relevant problems are we not able to solve with the tools we have acquired in this unit? What further complications do these problems add? What sorts of tools might help us to address them?

Problems and additional tools: Most units on differential calculus include a discussion of the anti-derivative, which leads naturally into integral calculus. Our purpose here is not to teach students integral calculus—that makes for another unit entirely—but to make them aware of the sorts of problems that differential calculus is unable to solve that can be addressed by integral calculus. We may also want to indicate the sorts of problems that could only be solved once students have learned differential equations.

The most obvious point is that students now know how to find the slope of a curve, but do not know how to find the area under a curve. To make this lack of knowledge pertinent, it might be useful to give some examples of the kinds of problems that can be solved by determining the area under a curve, and show how this set of problems relates closely to the kinds of problems students have learned to solve with differential calculus. If we have taught students about the anti-derivative, we can show how that tool can serve as a starting point for the more involved methods of integral calculus.

5. Encouraging Development of the Students' Sense of Agency. *What features of the knowledge will best allow us to encourage the students' developing sense of agency?*

Areas in which students' sense of agency can be engaged and encouraged: Learning differential calculus is not exactly a spur to get students writing letters to their local elected official, but it does provide a greater sense of control over a subject that is very stressful to young adults: change. There are a number of ways to highlight the relevance of this newfound mastery over a very abstract subject to the world around them. As noted earlier, change is ubiquitous, and all change can, with greater or lesser relevance, be expressed as a polynomial function. The class might enjoy the challenge of finding an example of change that is most resistant to graphical representation—followed by a challenge to find a means of graphing it. A further exercise might invite students to graph the function of some non-mathematical kind of change—the brightness of the teacher's apparent mood as a function of time over the course of a day, for example—and then to draw the derivative of that graph and try to explain what the derivative represents. The point of these kinds of exercises is primarily to give students a sense of agency with regard to the changes in their lives. While calculus itself may not help them deal with their romantic troubles, a greater sense of confidence in recognizing and analyzing change just might.

6. Conclusion. *How can we ensure that the students have grasped not only a new set of theoretical tools but also an understanding of where these tools fit into a larger conceptual framework? How can we ensure that the students understand not only how to apply what they have learned, but also why it works and why it should matter that they understand it?*

Concluding activity: This might be a good point to return to the historical narrative about the discovery of calculus by Newton and Leibniz and the central place of calculus in bringing about a new worldview from the old medieval order. We could challenge students to think of problems that cannot be solved without calculus, which highlight the limitations of the worldview in which such problems had to be left unsolved. The class could brainstorm a list of the kinds of solutions to problems and the kinds of inventions that would not have been possible without calculus. These exercises might lead into further reflection on how our own assumptions about the world around us are influenced by the mathematical tools our culture makes available to us.

7. Evaluation. *How can we know whether the content has been learned and understood, whether students have developed a theory or general idea, elaborated it, and attained some sense of its limitations?*

Forms of evaluation: Unpleasant as it is, repetition is one of the best ways to reinforce a basic command of the mathematical tools without which calculus is nothing more than a nice idea. Though exercises, homework, and quizzes are obviously useful in this regard, these well-used methods of evaluation only give a sense of students' mastery of the tools for doing calculus. We need further methods of evaluation to monitor the extent to which students have absorbed these mathematical tools into a broader understanding of where they belong in overall conceptual frameworks. The students' grasp of these broader themes might emerge through exercises normally anathema to a math class, such as essays, class discussion, and open debate. Some of the exercises suggested as ways for students to relate their technical mastery of differential calculus to a broader understanding of change might also serve as useful means of evaluating progress.

Example Three: Hamlet

1. Identifying Powerful Underlying Ideas. *What underlying ideas or theories seem best able to organize the topic into some coherent whole?*

What are the most powerful, clear, and relevant theories, ideologies, metaphysical schemes, or meta-narratives?

For "Hamlet," as far as teaching is concerned, "the play's the thing." What the framework can do is, indeed, *frame* the play, so that students' access and understanding can be increased. The trick is to engage students in the theories about the play that have hovered around it for hundreds of years. It is the most celebrated play in the English language, yet also one of the most argued about. So the theories that have been debated so intently can form a framework to engage the students in the play itself. "Hamlet" can appear quite daunting, as coming from the mind of a god rather than a living person, if presented as the most canonical piece of the canon. There are many ways one can try to move into the play while preventing it from becoming incomprehensible because so canonical—the way it is difficult to "see" the Mona Lisa because its canonical status blinds the viewer to the details of the painting itself. One might, for example, tell a story, set in modern times, that captures some central part of "Hamlet" and ask the students how they might go about staging that. Get them to do some dialogue work, then improvise a scene. One might then move to Shakespeare's version. This wouldn't necessarily make the play less overwhelming, but it might help the students to begin to think of it as living drama rather than as a petrified chunk of "unseeable" canonical Art. It may also help them to see that Shakespeare worked to deal with problems not unlike the ones they face.

The most powerful underlying idea or theory in this topic: This is one of the most celebrated dramas ever written, yet people endlessly dispute what it is about and why it is so celebrated. The unit will focus on why this story of revenge becomes so complicated, and why some think it is a dramatic failure and others a success. And behind this question lies the larger problem of what is drama, and why pretend-action on the stage can grip us so: "What's Hecuba to him or he to Hecuba / That he should weep for her?" Many theories offer themselves as bases on which to structure this unit. This example adopts the theory that "Hamlet" is successful as a drama because it shows the central character driven by a variety of competing impulses and forces that would propel him to action if any one of them became dominant at any point; the audience is caught by the tension of whether and when he might break free, and what he might do.

An *alternative*: It is a Renaissance thriller—will Hamlet kill the king first or will the king kill Hamlet?

2. Organizing the Content into a Theoretic Structure. This is a two-step process:

2.1. Initial Access. How can the underlying theory or idea be made vivid? What content best exposes it and shows its power to organize the topic?

Content that exposes the scheme or theory most vividly: The teacher might begin by giving an overview of the plot. The prince's wish to revenge his father's murder at the hands of his uncle is complicated by his mother's marriage to that uncle. The prince wants vengeance, is torn by his love of his mother, is ultimately uncertain of the "evidence" he is given—from a ghost, is full of passion and thoughts of revenge and love and friendship but is generally uncertain of anything. He is having difficulty separating "seems" from "is." So the discussion can begin with Hamlet's speech about the visiting players, in Act II, Scene II.

> *O! what a rogue and peasant slave am I:*
> *Is it not monstrous that this player here,*
> *But in a fiction, in a dream of passion,*
> *Could force his soul so to his own conceit*
> *That from her working all his visage wann'd,*
> *Tears in his eyes, distraction in 's aspect,*
> *A broken voice, and his whole function suiting*
> *With forms to his conceit? and all for nothing!*
> *For Hecuba!*
> *What's Hecuba to him or he to Hecuba*
> *That he should weep for her? What would he do*

Had he the motive and the cue for passion
That I have? He would drown the stage with tears,
And cleave the general ear with horrid speech,
Make mad the guilty and appal the free,
Confound the ignorant, and amaze indeed
The very faculties of eyes and ears.
Yet I,
A dull and muddy-mettled rascal, peak,
Like John-a-dreams, unpregnant of my cause,
And can say nothing; no, not for a king,
Upon whose property and most dear life
A damn'd defeat was made. Am I a coward?
Who calls me villain? breaks my pate across?
Plucks off my beard and blows it in my face?
Tweaks me by the nose? gives me the lie i' the throat,
As deep as to the lungs? Who does me this?
Ha!
Swounds, I should take it, for it cannot be
But I am pigeon-liver'd, and lack gall
To make oppression bitter, or ere this
I should have fatted all the region kites
With this slave's offal. Bloody, bawdy villain!
Remorseless, treacherous, lecherous, kindless villain!
O! vengeance!
Why, what an ass am I! This is most brave
That I, the son of a dear father murder'd,
Prompted to my revenge by heaven and hell,
Must, like a whore, unpack my heart with words,
And fall a-cursing, like a very drab,
A scullion!
Fie upon't! foh! About, my brain! I have heard,
That guilty creatures sitting at a play
Have by the very cunning of the scene
Been struck so to the soul that presently
They have proclaim'd their malefactions;

For murder, though it have no tongue, will speak
With most miraculous organ. I'll have these players
Play something like the murder of my father
Before mine uncle; I'll observe his looks;
I'll tent him to the quick: if he but blench
I know my course. The spirit that I have seen
May be the devil: and the devil hath power
To assume a pleasing shape; yea, and perhaps
Out of my weakness and my melancholy—
As he is very potent with such spirits—
Abuses me to damn me. I'll have grounds
More relative than this: the play's the thing
Wherein I'll catch the conscience of the king.

The first lesson can be spent with this speech, and the students can be asked, "What's the problem with this guy?" They will have the outline of the story, and here can focus on many of the central themes of the play. Why does he feel self-loathing at his inability to act? Are his desire for vengeance and his sense of justice at war? But why does he compare himself poorly with the actor's easy emotion? Is the artificiality of that emotion connected with his own uncertainties? The actor has only to express feeling. Hamlet also thinks.

It might be useful at this point to see the scene in some video format, starting with the entry of the players in one of the better versions—Kenneth Branagh's film is as good as any, and better than most.

2.2. Organizing the Body of the Lesson or Unit. What meta-narrative provides a clear overall structure to the lesson or unit?

Content that will present a strong meta-narrative of the topic: A few class periods could usefully be spent seeing the play at this point, in two different renderings. Olivier's old and now seemingly mannered version might make a good contrast to Branagh's. Apart from the radical truncation of the text in one and the whole text in the other, the contrast of the two interpretations can be brought to focus on the question of whether or not the play "works" in some coherent sense or whether it is the mysterious inadequacies of motivated action that draw people into it. And students can be asked to decide where the action of the play resides—in the world or in Hamlet's head—and whether these two are well coordinated.

The meta-narrative that follows from this guiding theory about the success of the play directs us to see all its features as masterfully working together; each element, each scene, each character will be interpreted as successful and as contributing to a coherent whole.

3. Introducing Anomalies to the Theory. *What content is anomalous to the general idea or theory? How can one begin with minor anomalies and gradually and sensitively challenge the students' general theory so that they make the theory increasingly sophisticated?*

Main anomalies to the meta-narrative: Here the point is to raise questions about whether the play is so flawlessly constructed as the meta-narrative insists. The teacher might ask students what they would do in Hamlet's place. If they propose a clear line of action— say, kill off the king early on, or certainly in that unguarded moment of prayer, the teacher can pose the various reasons why this would be an unsatisfactory solution. Against prompt murder, the teacher might raise the practical problems of getting at a well-guarded and suspicious king, and the psychological problem of Hamlet's uncertainty about whether his uncle did actually kill his father. Against taking advantage of the moment of prayer, Hamlet wants to see his uncle rot in hell, so resists killing him when he is seemingly repentant and in a state approaching grace. To make this plausible to students today, the teacher might have to work a little at conveying the conception of hell at the time.

On the more general question of whether or not the play works as drama, the teacher can be prepared with the arguments on either side. Good preparation for the position that takes exception to the meta-narrative and its governing theory would be T.S. Eliot's essay "Hamlet and His Problems," in which he argues that the emotion of the play is out of tune with the action; there is no adequate "objective correlative" for the emotion in the actions, and so the play leaves a feeling of dissatisfaction. For Eliot, and many others, the play is the problem rather than the psyche of its leading character. (There are many easy sources for this short and interesting essay today, such as www.bartleby.com/200/sw9.html.)

Those students who take the position that Hamlet is disabled by thinking too much—a victim of the "pale cast of thought"— might be asked to consider his decisive and ruthless action with regard to the deceitful Rosencrantz and Guildenstern. And he is clearly thought to be a "man of action" as evidenced by his skill with a sword, even though a scholar, and also in that Fortinbras insists on a soldier's funeral for him, with full honors. Do the decisive Hamlet and the indecisive Hamlet constitute a coherent character?

And those that wonder about his madness, especially in his dealings with Ophelia, might be asked to reflect on his fear that the king might kill him and has been subverting his friends, and clearly Ophelia, to betray him. But are his dealings with Ophelia not overwrought and—anomalously to our meta-narrative—unsatisfactory? And can't one complain that much the same can be said about his other relationships? Isn't the emotion out of proportion and the action contrived?

There is no shortage of anomalies to any position taken on Hamlet. One must, in the end, conclude that Shakespeare was simply smarter than we are—or that Shakespeare was writing a potboiler to fill the cultural niche now occupied by TV cop shows and didn't feel any need to resolve this stuff.

4. Presenting Alternative General Theories. *What alternative general theories can organize the topic? What alternative meta-narrative can organize the topic? Which can best be used to help students see something about the nature and limitations of their theories and meta-narratives?*

Alternative theories or meta-narratives: The teacher could ask the students to imagine what the first audiences of the play might have seen in it. Several earlier "Hamlet" plays had been staged, including a recent one by Thomas Kyd, and the story appears in chronicles that Shakespeare and his audiences would have known. But Shakespeare changed the old revenge formula into something amazingly more complex and engaging. What about the notion of a thriller, in which the gripping part of the plot is not our fascination with Hamlet's psyche, which we can indulge because we know what is going to happen, but rather, for the person who sees the play for a first time, who is going to kill whom first?

But the primary meta-narrative explains the play's power to grip people as due to masterful alignment of the elements to make a seamless whole. The teacher can thus ask the students to think of flawed works of art that nevertheless have a power to grip their imaginations and can ask them to reflect on whether "Hamlet" isn't the most successful failure ever to be performed.

Then there are aspects of the "What's Hecuba to him?" question. The teacher can solicit students' views on this, and ask them to compare their ideas with Hamlet's own musings in the speech quoted at the beginning. Why should the player weep for Hecuba and we for Hamlet?

Then there's always the "It's just all a bit too much" theory; that a sensitive person under the array of stresses that pound Hamlet just finds his brain whirring as he tries to deal with it all. Life, death, love, and intense fear—enough to make a lad long for the days playing with Yorik.

5. Encouraging Development of the Students' Sense of Agency. *What features of the knowledge will best allow us to encourage the students' developing sense of agency?*

Areas in which students' sense of agency can be engaged and encouraged: One of the uses of literature is to expand our experience, to take on others' experience as though it is our own and learn from it. Seriously following "Hamlet" is itself an enlargement of the students' sense of agency.

Giving students roles to play—as is suggested in the next section—will also allow them to "try on" a persona and imagine themselves, or rather imagine a self they might move toward or come to inhabit, as like that persona. Suggest to students that during a day, when it would not be too disruptive, they might "be" Hamlet, or Ophelia, or Gertrude, Polonius, or one of the others. Think of their role in the basketball game as themselves being Ophelia or Gertrude, Hamlet or Laertes, or moving through the mall or riding the bus or being in class at school. How would those characters do such things? How would the students expand their sense of self imagining how they would do such things? Of course, these characters' realization is only within the play, but it might be an interesting exercise to embody them in some form in modern contexts, as one sees playful students do with characters from movies.

6. Conclusion. *How can we ensure that the students' theories or general ideas are not destroyed but are recognized as having a different status from the facts they are based on? How can we ensure that the decay of belief in the Truth of theories or general ideas does not lead to disillusion and alienation?*

Concluding activity: The play is designed to be performed and watched rather than read, though readers have the stage of their minds to perform the play in. For the conclusion it might help students get closer to some of the questions that have been buzzing around their study of the play by having them prepare performances. They might break up into small groups and choose a number of key scenes in the play, allotting these scenes to different groups, ensuring that each student will have a role. The best scenes are those in which personal relationships and their dynamics are central to the action. Hamlet with Gertrude, Hamlet with Guildenstern and Rosencrantz (or was it . . . ?), Hamlet with Ophelia, Ophelia with Polonius and the king, and so on.

The students should learn their roles by heart. (This seems to run against many teachers' assumption that "rote learning" is somehow damaging. Yet Shakespeare's work amounts to one of the great "supertools" for individuals' cognitive development, and learning the rhythms of his language and psyche and emotions constitutes one of the greatest contributors to students' education. This benefit comes most fully when his words are learned by heart.)

The students would then perform their scenes for the full class, and for any others who might attend, and discuss their conclusions about the theoretical issues surrounding the play from their experience in rehearsals. As each group will have had more close attention to the text and more intense emotional involvement with some of the characters, these concluding discussions of the general ideas about "Hamlet" should be better informed and more subtle than earlier attempts to articulate and defend particular theories about the play.

7. Evaluation. *How can we know whether the content has been learned and understood, whether students have developed a theory or general idea, elaborated it, and attained some sense of its limitations?*

Forms of evaluation: Any of the usual forms of evaluation can be used to assess to what degree students have understood the text, know the plot, and so on. In addition to those usual forms of assessment, the teacher will also want to seek evidence that students have understood and developed for themselves theories about the play. Evidence of their theoretical understanding can come from observations of their performances and discussions about them and from assigned essay topics that allow students to explore and articulate theories they have begun to develop during the unit. And as the overarching objective is to engage the students with "Hamlet" rather than with theories about the play, it would be helpful to seek some evidence from their work and essays that this objective has not become subverted by the means we have used to achieve it.

Example Four: Simple Harmonic Motion (Ages Sixteen to Eighteen)

Oscillation is nature's way of restoring equilibrium. The process of restoring this equilibrium gives rise to many significant natural phenomena, not least of which are light and sound waves. While oscillation can be a very complicated process, its basics as found in simple harmonic motion are not hard to master. This two-to-three-week unit examines the tools necessary to analyze simple harmonic motion and explores their surprisingly wide-ranging application.

1. *Identifying Powerful Underlying Ideas.* *What underlying ideas or theories seem best able to organize the topic into some coherent whole? What are the most powerful, clear, and relevant theories, ideologies, metaphysical schemes, or meta-narratives?*

The most powerful underlying idea or theory in this topic: Oscillation is nature's way of finding equilibrium. When a system is thrown out of equilibrium, it gains an excess of energy that must somehow be shed before it can return to equilibrium. This process of shedding energy produces such disparate phenomena as ocean and sound waves. The interplay between equilibrium and disequilibrium is everywhere in nature, and without it we would be able neither to see nor to hear.

An alternative: The motion of a mass on a spring can be graphed with the same functions that describe the coordinates at various points on a circle. Harmonic motion in general is *sinusoidal*, meaning that the properties of the mysterious, perfect circle find their way into a variety of natural phenomena that we do not normally associate with circles. An alternative approach to this unit might involve investigating the ways in which the properties of the circle are present everywhere in nature.

2. *Organizing the Content into a Theoretic Structure.* This is a two-step process:

2.1. Initial Access. *How can the underlying theory or idea be made vivid? What content best exposes it and shows its power to organize the topic?*

Content that exposes the scheme or theory most vividly: The paradigmatic example of simple harmonic motion is the mass on a spring, partly because it reveals the properties of harmonic motion so plainly and partly because it is so conducive to in-class demonstrations. You might begin by demonstrating the motion of a mass suspended from a spring, showing how it oscillates about an equilibrium point until it comes to rest, and then brainstorm as many seemingly dissimilar phenomena that also exhibit these simple properties of oscillation and equilibrium. They appear in everything from waves on water to the vibrations of a guitar string to the changes in populations of predators and prey in ecosystems. Students can also learn that light and sound travel in oscillating waves, and that vision and hearing are possible by the way membranes in our body respond to these oscillations.

From these observations, students can investigate what all these phenomena have in common, beginning with the equilibrium point and oscillation about that equilibrium. They might also address such basic questions as whether oscillation happens at a steady speed, or whether the speed is greater at the equilibrium point or at the maximum displacement from the equilibrium point. They might also ask what sorts of forces must be at work such that something might oscillate about a point of equilibrium without either coming immediately to rest at the point of equilibrium or displacing itself indefinitely away from the point of equilibrium. The goal in this unit will be to develop the mathematical tools that help students formalize the commonality between all these phenomena of oscillation, giving them a clear grasp of how all these disparate phenomena share a few simple mathematical properties.

2.2 Organizing the Body of the Lesson or Unit. What meta-narrative provides a clear overall structure to the lesson or unit?

Content that will present a strong meta-narrative of the topic: The big story here is that nature is in a constant interplay between seeking a state of equilibrium and having that equilibrium interrupted. Neither equilibrium nor disequilibrium are themselves of as much interest as the oscillation between them. The sound of music and the oceans' tides are the results of systems oscillating about their point of equilibrium. If these systems were ever to find their point of equilibrium or if they were suspended permanently in some state away from their point of equilibrium they would cease to be interesting.

One interesting tension in this story is the way in which oscillation is simply a by-product of a system out of equilibrium trying to restore its equilibrium, but it is this by-product that produces the most interesting results. The vibrations of a guitar string are simply the result of the string trying to return to the state it was in before it was plucked, but it is these vibrations—not the plucking or the equilibrium state—that produce the sound. The teacher might want to highlight the romance of this ugly duckling notion, that what seems to be the uninteresting process of getting from one state to another is in fact more important than either of the two states.

3. Developing the Tools to Analyze the Theoretic Structure. *What mathematical or scientific tools will help us analyze the phenomena touched upon in the general idea or theory? How can we develop and explore these tools in a way that underlines their pertinence to the general idea or theory?*

Major tools and their pertinence: After exploring the wide variety of oscillations present in nature, the teacher may want to return to the original mass-on-a-spring example where the various mathematical properties of simple harmonic motion are most evident. By studying the relationship between displacement and velocity in a mass-on-a-spring system, the class can derive Hooke's Law, as well as the various formulas expressing the period, amplitude, displacement, velocity, acceleration, and potential and kinetic energy of an object undergoing simple harmonic motion.

In examining the general properties of simple harmonic motion, it would also be worthwhile to examine the relationship between harmonic motion and sinusoidal functions. In this way, students can see that the properties of simple harmonic motion are related to the even simpler properties of the circle. In the supreme generality of the circle they will find applications in almost every aspect of nature.

4. Taking Account of the Limitations of the Theoretic Structure. *What relevant problems are we not able to solve with the tools we have acquired in this unit? What further complications do these problems add? What sorts of tools might help us to address them?*

Problems and additional tools: Here is where the *simple* and the *harmonic* parts of "simple harmonic motion" come into play. A common example given in a unit on simple harmonic motion is that of pendulum motion. Although pendulum motion bears many useful analogies to simple harmonic motion, however, it is not an example of simple harmonic motion. It might be interesting to introduce pendulum motion by asking students whether pendulum motion is an example of simple harmonic motion and challenging them to prove whether it is or not.

Beyond the example of the pendulum, it might be worth showing students that almost all oscillations in nature are not as simple as the mass on a spring. Using the mathematical tools acquired earlier, they can discover that an object displaced from its equilibrium position will have greater energy, so that oscillation is essentially a matter of shedding the excess energy that prevents it from returning to rest at its equilibrium position. This never happens in simple harmonic motion because the assumption there is that nothing will dissipate the energy. In real life, however, most oscillation comes to a stop unless some force keeps it going. For example, a mass on a spring will stop oscillating because the stiffness of the spring and friction will dissipate energy as heat, allowing the mass to return to its equilibrium position. Making sense of these more complicated forms of oscillation will require mathematics beyond what is covered in this unit.

Without delving into the complicated mathematics, the teacher can show how damped, driven, and self-exciting oscillations complicate the simple formulas covered earlier in this unit. It is also worth noting the usefulness of these further kinds of oscillation. A pertinent example is the damping of the shocks on a car. If the bounces in a car obeyed the laws of simple harmonic motion, passengers would be in for a very rough ride indeed, so auto engineers have damped the shocks in cars to minimize the bounciness.

5. *Encouraging Development of the Students' Sense of Agency.**
What features of the knowledge will best allow us to encourage the students' developing sense of agency?

Areas in which students' sense of agency can be engaged and encouraged: In the abstract generality of math and physics, students can discover a feeling of agency at grasping the fundamentals behind a wide array of seemingly disparate phenomena. Studying oscillation, for example, can help students develop a sense of how they can analyze and make sense of a wide array of problems and reduce seemingly complicated behavior to a few simple terms and equations. It might engage the students' sense of agency to find as many different examples of oscillation as they can in their own lives and to invent formulas that express the "force" or "potential energy" at the various points in these oscillations. Such oscillations need not just be obvious examples like music or bouncing basketballs. Oscillation finds its way into the human world as well, in the fluctuation in popularity of entertainers, the way large groups of people move to occupy space in a mall, and many other social phenomena.

6. Conclusion. *How can we ensure that the students have grasped not only a new set of theoretical tools, but also an understanding of where these tools fit into a larger conceptual framework? How can we ensure that the students understand not only how to apply what they have learned, but also why it works and why it should matter that they understand it?*

Concluding activity: A useful activity at this point might be to return to the list brainstormed at the beginning of the unit of the many different ways in which oscillation manifests itself in nature. Drawing on the mass-on-a-spring example, students can seek analogies for the various terms such as force, displacement, or kinetic energy as they apply to examples of oscillation in which these terms are inappropriate. Obviously, the oscillations in population between predator and prey in an ecosystem don't involve velocity or acceleration, but students can examine how these kinematic properties have clear analogues in biology, sound production, and elsewhere. This analysis will help the class perceive how this relatively simple set of mathematical tools has tremendously wide-ranging application.

6. Evaluation. *How can we know whether the content has been learned and understood, whether students have developed a theory or general idea, elaborated it, and attained some sense of its limitations?*

Forms of evaluation: To gain a firm grasp of the mathematical tools involved in analyzing simple harmonic motion, students will need to do a certain amount of repetitive drilling, both as in-class exercises and as homework, and then have their mastery of these tools evaluated in standard tests. Understanding the wide-ranging importance of simple harmonic motion is useless if students cannot also understand the mathematics with which to analyze this important phenomenon. However, understanding the mathematics is equally useless if students do not understand its pertinence. Exercises suggested here challenge students to find examples of harmonic motion in their own lives, and to find analogies for the mechanical terms in the mass-on-a-spring example as applied to other instances of oscillation. These exercises should make it possible to evaluate the grasp students have of the general principles of simple harmonic motion, and the extent to which its principles can be applied.

Conclusion

Imagination Every Day

Thank you for trudging through to the end with me—unless you are one of those people who start at the back, to see who dunnit, in which case, welcome!

I hope you will agree that I've carried through with the perhaps overly bold claim of being able to help teachers engage students' imaginations in learning about algebra, history, and so on throughout the years of schooling. I have used frameworks derived from sets of cognitive tools that students have available to use for learning:

- For the youngest children: These children have already acquired the great tool kit of oral language, and they learn most easily when we use those tools—story, metaphor, binary opposites, rhyme, rhythm, and pattern, jokes and humor, mental imagery, gossip, play, and the sense of mystery—in helping them learn about their world. They are beginning to develop the tools of literacy, and lessons can help them grow in that direction without assuming they've already mastered those tools.

- For children in middle years: The tools of orality remain effective, but a whole new set develops along with literacy—the sense of reality, the pursuit of extremes of experience and limits of reality, association with heroes, the sense of wonder, the relationship of knowledge and human meaning, narrative understanding, revolt and idealism, changing the context, and the literate eye. We need to help them exercise and exploit these tools. In addition, many are beginning to develop the tools of theoretic thinking, and we can encourage that growth.

209

- For adolescents and young adults: The tools of literacy have joined those of orality, and some students are developing a third set related to theoretic thinking—they are developing a sense of abstract reality, a sense of agency, and a grasp of general ideas and their anomalies, and they search for authority and truth and begin to build meta-narrative understanding—while others need help in recognizing the usefulness of these modes of working with the world. And some are beginning to move on, discovering ways in which theoretic thinking fails to capture the reality it is supposed to represent or explain; they are developing an "ironic" perspective, but the tool kit of ironic understanding is beyond the scope of this book (see Egan, 1997, if you are interested in what it looks like).

The formulas and frameworks I have presented are, as I have emphasized throughout, not there to be slavishly followed. Rather they are designed as simple reminders of the principles of imaginative engagement that they try to embody. Once you become sufficiently familiar with the principles, to the point that you apply them routinely in thinking about how to teach a topic, then the frameworks become dispensable. As I have said a few times, they are a crutch, to be used only as long as needed.

And, of course, I don't think I have been describing the only way to plan for imaginative teaching. This is a schematic for capturing a fairly wide array of tools, but it omits many many other ways of doing the job. I do think, though, when I hear of particularly imaginative teaching, that some of the cognitive tools described here are usually in play. But the variety of ways that such tools can be used is enormous, and I have barely scratched the surface.

David—the son who wrote two examples in the preceding chapter—also sent me, along with helpful criticism of my "Hamlet" example, the following e-mail message:

I was reading over a book on improvization yesterday and came across two anecdotes I thought you might like.

The first is about Benjamin Constant's tutor deciding, when Constant was five, that they'd invent a new language. So the tutor took Constant outside and started inventing names for all the different things that they saw. Constant got very engaged in this process of finding new ways of saying things, and gradually they developed a whole grammar for this new language and even a new writing system to express sounds in the language. It wasn't until Constant was six that he discovered that he'd learned Ancient Greek.

The other was that Einstein was taught that algebra is all about a hunt for a creature called X, and when you catch it, it has to tell you its name.

Now clearly Constant and Einstein had unusual intellects, but we may wonder whether they would have been quite so extraordinary if their teachers hadn't engaged their imaginations and enhanced the power of the cognitive tools they had picked up. And, oddly enough, they managed all this without using my frameworks! You might find the frameworks simply suggestive and not need them either, but there they are just in case anyone wants a more systematic way of trying this imaginative approach to teaching.

The soul of teaching has to do with meaning. Everyone concerned with education, from the beginning, has recognized that the task is not simply to teach facts and skills that can be reproduced when required. The trick is to tie the facts and skills to their deeper meaning in human experience. Throughout history, thinkers have tried to capture this essence of education in terms of images. Chuang-tzu long ago, in what is perhaps his best-known playful reflection, suggested that we are like a person who is asleep. In sleep that person may dream, and may even dream that he is dreaming. But when he wakes, he realizes that it was a dream. And so for each of us, perhaps some day there will be a great awakening when we will realize this everyday world was all just a strange dream. A little later, some way from Chuangtzu, another mystic, jokester, dreamer, and philosopher, Plato, suggested a similar image. Human life is like that of prisoners looking at the shadows on a wall, imagining that those shadows are all of reality. But, by releasing the prisoner within us, we can come to see that reality is more abundant and rich, and as different from the shadows of everyday experience as a dream is from reality.

The soul of teaching has to do with meaning.

These images are supposed to reflect the idea that our experience is constantly under threat of being impoverished by the conventions, routines, and anxieties of everyday living. One crucial purpose of education is the incessant struggle against the trivializing of our lives. The soul of teaching is this daily battle to enlarge, enrich, and make more abundant the experience of children. And crucial to this is engaging their imaginations in the world around them.

Yesterday I was reading a book about imagination and education and was astonished to find in it a quotation from something that Dan Nadaner and I wrote a number of years ago. I had been drafting some notes about how I would finish this book, emphasizing the centrality of imagination to everyday educational practice, and there was the old chunk of text that says just what I still want to say again:

> Imagination is not some desirable but dispensable frill, . . . it is the heart of any truly educational experience; it is not something split off from "the basics" or disciplined thought or rational inquiry, but is the quality that can give them life and meaning; it is not something belonging properly to the arts, but it is the pragmatic center of all effective human thinking. Our concern is not to promote imagination at the expense of something else—say, rational inquiry or the foundational "3Rs"; rather it is to show that any conception of rational inquiry or the foundations of education that depreciates imagination is impoverished and sure to be a practical failure. Stimulating the imagination is not an alternative educational activity to be argued for in competition with other claims; it is a prerequisite to making any activity educational [1988, p. ix].

I have given examples of the uses of each cognitive tool in everyday teaching, and then looked at how they can be brought together into a framework that can guide the planning of a lesson or unit of study. I have found that, as teachers become more familiar with this approach, they tend to try one or two of the tools in a lesson, then they try shaping a whole lesson or unit using one of the frameworks, and then, often in association with colleagues, they use one of the frameworks to plan a semester or year's work into which all the required curriculum material is fit. This last is perhaps the fullest and best use of this approach, as it can create quite dramatic and memorable experiences for students and teachers.

Now I may seem to have been making bold claims and promising a lot. But there is a problem. Changing to this form of imaginative teaching often turns out to be more difficult than it first appears. Perhaps I can indicate something of the problem some teachers have had by describing what tends to happen when I have given workshops on how to use the frameworks for planning.

Usually, teachers attending the workshops are persuaded that the approach is sensible. Often, of course, they are attracted to the workshops because they are already persuaded of this and are looking for practical help in how to engage students' imaginations in their everyday teaching. Indeed, I am usually a little surprised and pleased by how well the initial outline of the principles is accepted. A lot of teachers say, after I describe features of students' imaginations—as I do in this book—that this describes the students they teach, and that it captures features of their thinking and learning that the teachers have intuitively felt but not thought of quite like this. Often they say they have not focused on these features of learning because currently dominant planning models and the theories they have been required to read in textbooks guide them away from students' imaginative lives and almost exclusively toward students' logical abilities. The descriptions of students' imagination, they claim, capture much better what students are really like as learners.

You can imagine that I find these responses very gratifying. But then we come to the problem. What teachers typically find so refreshing is that when we examine imagination we are also dealing with some of the central features of students' emotional engagements with knowledge. That is, it is students' emotional responses that we are centrally concerned with, not just their conceptual grasp of the logic of content. But the main point I make is that for this alternative approach to work in the classroom, the teacher's own emotional engagement with the content must become central too. And that's where the workshops sometimes run into trouble.

After I have described the attractive package, as it were, I then ask teachers to plan a lesson according to one of the frameworks. In each of the three frameworks, the first item has nothing to do with objectives, nor with neatly organizing the content; it focuses on feelings. I introduce this practical part of the workshop by suggesting that unless teachers can identify in themselves some emotional response to the content, there is no way they can make it emotionally engaging to students.

Teachers commonly respond well to the suggestion that we should demechanize planning in education—all that "objectives" language is derived from industrial procedures, after all, not from human interactions. We should reemphasize its human dimensions and reemphasize that teaching is about communicating meanings more than it is about attaining objectives. These are not mutually exclusive alternatives, of course, but which we put first significantly determines what goes on in the classroom. And mostly teachers react well, if a little warily, to the suggestion that they must begin planning by considering the content to be taught in terms of their emotional response to it. But they rarely have any clear idea how to do this.

Part of the problem is that most teachers are very skilled at planning a topic in appropriate lesson-sized pieces; they are usually excellent at providing varied classroom activities to ensure the topic is learned; they are usually very competent at scheduling the content into a sequence that is logically comprehensible. Often, I think, nonteachers—and many teachers themselves—don't recognize the amount of very sophisticated skill that is daily deployed in planning and teaching a topic to a group of thirty or so very different children. In the process of gaining all this skill, however, the thing I am trying to make central to the process is typically given little or no practice or encouragement. So, naturally—but a bit to my surprise initially—teachers sometimes find it quite hard.

Another part of the problem is that teachers are sometimes skeptical that the kind of emotional engagement I am talking about is either possible or sensible. As one articulate pre-service teacher said in Pittsburgh recently when I got to the point in the workshop where I was asking them to find within themselves some emotional response to the topic they were to teach:

"You mean, you're saying that if I can't get emotionally turned on by fractions or punctuation, I can't teach them successfully?"

"Well, you may be successful in that you will get students to learn the material adequately to pass tests, but, yes, I am saying that you will likely be unable to engage the students' imaginations in the comma, and they won't remember it long and it will have no real meaning for them. If you do engage their imaginations, they will pass the test much more easily and with higher scores and also, which is more important, they will recognize why the comma matters."

"That doesn't make sense. How am I supposed to get emotional about fractions for one class, then punctuation for another, then some science. I'd be a wreck by the end of the day!"

"I think you'd be less of a wreck at the end of the day if you could identify the topic's emotional importance to you. It's what is at the core of meaning. Teachers who do find that emotional engagement typically find themselves energized rather than drained by the end of the day. And their classes have more children who are themselves imaginatively engaged, and that in turn energizes the teachers further."

Teachers who find emotional engagement typically find themselves energized rather than drained by the end of the day.

"I don't believe any of that makes sense."

I invited her to give it a try, suggesting we would work together on a topic and see whether we couldn't think about it in such a way that we could identify something about it that turned us on.

I did suggest that she might think of what I was asking her to do not so much as some complex intellectual act but rather as more like gossiping about the comma or about fractions. When we gossip— which is the oldest and easiest form of human verbal interaction— we organize information into narrative structures in order to convey the emotional meaning of the information. Good gossipers, or good *conversationalists*, to use a more polite term, are engaging. Good gossip doesn't exhaust one; rather it gives energy and pleasure. We began outlining a unit on the comma, which was later elaborated in another workshop with another teacher, and the end product may be seen at www.ierg.net/teach_la.html. She seemed quite pleased with the result and has since e-mailed to tell me how successful it has been with her class.

Here's the ambivalence, then, and the warning that should come with the three frameworks. On one hand, evoking the narrative imagination in learning is a much more "natural" way of learning effectively. On the other hand, when teachers' training and the institution of the school and the textbooks produced for students pay little attention to this crucial aspect of human ways of learning and making sense of the world, to suddenly begin to think in this significantly different way is often quite hard. It might seem attractive and desirable for all kinds of reasons, but that doesn't always make it easy.

Now, having put it so boldly, I should also add that I meet a lot of teachers who take to this alternative approach like ducks to water. It's as though they are released to be able to teach in ways that are much more harmonious with how they themselves think and make sense of the world. And this is my central claim about this general approach: that it is much better attuned to how we make sense of our everyday world and to how we learn about what really interests us and matters to us, than are the typical models currently on offer in textbooks about planning teaching.

You can find out more about this approach, and see other examples, and communicate with other teachers who are also trying this approach, or who have been using it for some years, by visiting the IERG Web site at www.ierg.net. You can also discuss this book with the author, ask questions, make critical comments, add your ideas at either www.educ.sfu.ca/kegan/ or at www.ierg.net/forums/.

Despite my brash claim that this book can demonstrate how to engage students' imaginations in learning, I do recognize this is just one in a line of books and articles struggling with the problem of how to make the daily experience of students in schools as imaginatively engaging as possible. And, of course, many thousands of teachers are daily doing just that in their own ways. So this book is just intended to be some help in that daily task, and I hope it will be found to have something to offer—even if that something is a bit less grand than my more manic self hopes for. I see the book not as some final statement or complete package: these are ideas I and the Imaginative Education Research Group and many others continue to work at. So think of the book as more like a part of a conversation about this educational challenge we all face. And please have your say, even if only in the limited forums offered on the Web sites I've mentioned. It is by each of us talking and learning from each other that will likely enable us to make more progress. In particular, the frameworks I have sketched might be much better designed. If you try them out and think of improvements, please let us know. (Indeed, as this book was in process of publication, Mark Fettes and Anne Chodakowski of IERG designed significantly improved frameworks. These frameworks have been inserted as Appendixes A, B, and C.)

Please have your say.

Glossary

Association with heroes: The tool that enables us to overcome some of the threat of alienation involved in the new sense of literate reality by allowing us to take on heroic qualities of those with whom we associate. It gives us the ability to imbue any aspect of reality with heightened importance.

Binary opposites: The most basic and powerful tools we have for organizing and categorizing the world, providing an initial ordering to many complex forms of knowledge.

Changing the context: A tool that enables the imagination to grasp the richer meaning of any topic by shifting the context in which it is learned.

Cognitive tools: Aids to thinking developed in human cultural history and learned by people today to enlarge their powers to think and understand.

Collections and hobbies: By putting immense intellectual energy into collecting a set of something or engaging in a hobby, students exercise their minds while satisfying an urge to securely understand something.

Embryonic tools: The tools of each level—orality, literacy, theoretic thinking—begin to take shape at the preceding level, and teachers need to provide opportunities for students to begin using them.

Extremes and limits of reality: The most exotic and bizarre phenomena, and the most terrible and courageous events.

Gossip: One of the most basic forms of social interaction—easy to engage in and usually pleasurable—that provides practice in fitting events into a narrative and develops oral language capacities.

Grasp of general ideas and their anomalies: The tool that allows students to generate abstract ideas about nature, society, history, and human psychology—and then to recognize their inadequacy and rebuild them into more complex ideas.

Imagination: The ability to think of things as possible—the source of flexibility and originality in human thinking. The literate imagination is enhanced by the array of discoveries and inventions made in cultural history.

Jokes and humor: Tool that exposes some of the basic ways in which language works and, at the same time, allows students to play with elements of knowledge, so discovering some of learning's rewards.

Knowledge and human meaning: The tool that goes beyond the surface of any knowledge to its source in human emotion.

Literacy: The set of cognitive tools available to us as we become literate; these cognitive tools do not automatically develop with learning to read and write, but they are tied to the students' learning to repeat within themselves the achievements of literacy in our cultural history.

Literate eye: The ability to pull information easily from texts and such symbolic forms as the list, flowchart, and diagram, reflecting a shift from dominance of the ear to the eye in gathering information.

Mental imagery: Unique images generated from words, which can carry more imaginative and memorable force than any description of the concept they represent.

Meta-narrative understanding: The tool that shapes knowledge into more general structures that permit a theoretical grasp of, and an emotional association with, the knowledge.

Metaphor: A tool that enlarges understanding by allowing the user to see one thing in terms of another.

Mystery: A tool that creates an attractive sense of how much that is fascinating remains to be discovered, drawing students' minds into the adventure of learning.

Narrative understanding: The tool that helps us make sense of things by grasping their emotional meaning, which applies to physics or mathematics no less than to history or literature.

Orality: The set of cognitive tools available to oral language users before literacy becomes fluent.

Play: A set of cognitive tools that helps people enlarge their understanding of the norms and limits of behavior and enlarge their self-control while getting pleasure from the pretence.

Revolt and idealism: Using these tools, students both resist the adult world and shift to find a place within it. Revolt implies an ideal, whose absence justifies the revolt.

Rhyme, rhythm, and pattern: Tools for giving meaningful, memorable, and attractive shape to any content.

Search for authority and truth: The tool used to attempt to determine which ideas are true, seeking an objective, certain, privileged view of reality.

Sense of abstract reality: The rational, logically structured form of thinking that enables students to make sense of the world in terms of abstract ideas.

Sense of agency: Recognition of the self as related to the world via complex causal chains and networks, permitting a realistic understanding of how people play roles in the real world and are products of historical and social processes.

Sense of reality: The ability to apply disembedded, rational, logically structured forms of thinking to information, including abstract processes.

Sense of wonder: The ability to focus on any aspect of the world around us, or the world within us, and see and enjoy its particular uniqueness.

Story: Narrative line that shapes real-world content as well as fictional material.

Theoretic thinking: The ability to develop theoretic abstractions and to use the other cognitive tools to that purpose.

Appendix A

Mythic Framework

Mythic Framework   Topic:

Finding a Narrative

Emotional Engagement	Central Image or Metaphor	Organizing Content into Story Form
What is emotionally engaging about the topic? How is it meaningful? Why should it matter to us?	*What content most dramatically illustrates the contrast between the binary opposite? Is there a metaphor or image that can do this?*	*How can we organize the content into a developing story form?*
This is a tough part, but there is something deeply meaningful about just about everything. What do you want students to gain from this unit or lesson? Years from now, what do you want them to remember?	Images are more than just pictures in the mind's eye; images can be made in all sensory modalities: visual, auditory, tactile, gustatory (taste), olfactory (smell), and perhaps even other senses that are not quite as easily described.	This is the trickiest part, and the part requiring the most imagination.
What binary concepts best capture the meaning and emotion of the topic? If this were a story, what would the opposing forces be?	Try to think of metaphors or images that capture the binary opposites that are moving the story forward.	"If you think of the lesson or unit as more like telling a good story than conveying a body of information, then the need to focus on how to tell the story as crisply as possible comes to the fore rather than the attempt to meet sets of knowledge, skills, and attitude objectives. If the story is told well, such objectives will be met in a more meaningful context" (Egan, *The Educated Mind*, p. 248).
We are looking for abstract polarities here such as love/hate, good/evil, rich/poor, friend/enemy, foolish/wise, hardworking/lazy…		Reflect on the whole unit or lesson and think of it in terms of some overall narrative structure. You want to select and highlight content that will make clear to students that one is not simply relating a sequence of facts or events, but that one has a story to tell them and that the set of facts and events have a unity of some kind.
		If you have listed a dozen possible binary opposites, pare it down to just one pair that will guide the unit. Decide which elements in the content fit best into the narrative and disregard the rest. Although it is hard to let go, it is crucial to remove unnecessary items that are not within the context of the story.

Developing Cognitive Tools

Images and Metaphor	Rhythm, Rhyme and Patterns	Drama and Roleplay
	Student-led/open-ended ⟵⟶ Teacher-led/structured	
What activities help students develop images, metaphors, or other forms of creative depiction?	*What activities help students experience and extend a sense of rhythm, rhyme, or predictability?*	*How can the students become characters in the story? How can they be encouraged and supported to contribute to or retell the story using their own words, gestures, and actions?*
What activities promote affective engagement with images or metaphors central to the story? How can students develop and experience metaphors such as these for themselves?	*What type of repetition or rhythm is inherent in the topic?*	If at all possible, make the students the main characters in the story, or find a way for them to get to know the characters (whether human, animal, mineral, or even something more abstract).
What jokes or fantastic stories can be found or invented that relate to the topic?	Look for patterns and rhythms not only in sight and sound, but also in a physical sense or in time and emotion. There is a rhythm in the rising and setting of the sun every day, and there is also a sense of rhythm in our hopes and fears. It is this sense of emotional rhythm that often drives good stories.	An example: A group of students can imagine they are squares, while another group imagines they are circles.
Jokes are close cousins to metaphors and are also an excellent way to reach deeper understanding when used wisely.	*What kinds of games, songs, activities, etc., let students have an embodied sense of the content's rhythm?*	

Looking Forward and Concluding

Toward Further Understanding	Resolution	Assessment
How can the unit develop embryonic forms of Romantic, Philosophic, and Ironic understanding? What cognitive tools characteristic of literacy, the disciplines, or embodied self-awareness can be introduced here?	*How does the story end? How are the opposites mediated or resolved?*	*How can one know whether the topic has been understood, its importance grasped, and the content learned?*
Consider questions that one might ask from a Romantic, Philosophic, or Ironic point-of-view. These might be presented to students as "brain candy," throughout the unit or toward its end, or they might become more substantial areas of inquiry. Remember that students do not "graduate" from one layer of understanding and move suddenly into the next. Rather, they will most likely experience a gradual shift in tendency toward or proficiency with particular cultural tools.	Decide what it is that you want the students to gain from the unit and how it relates to the binary opposites. You may or may not choose to reveal this to the children.	*How do you want to gather the information needed to know if you are successful?*
	Perhaps the villain turns out to be not as bad as once thought, or perhaps there is a realization that a marble, though tiny for us, would be quite large to a flea.	Don't forget about ongoing and mid-lesson or mid-unit assessment so that you can make necessary adaptations to the lesson or unit if needed.
(A unit at the Mythic level, however, will consistently emphasize and develop the cognitive tools of oral language even when some later tools are being introduced.)	Sometimes there is no mediation between the polarities, but a gradual move from one to the other. For example, on a unit on the environment where the binary opposites are despair and hope, you will want to make sure that the story ends on a feeling of hope rather than despair.	You can use traditional forms of evaluation, portfolios, rubrics, artwork, journal writing, or whatever else you think will be useful to gather the information needed to assess how well the students' imaginations have been engaged by the topic.

Appendix B

Romantic Framework

Romantic Framework   Topic:

Finding a Narrative

Heroic Qualities	Heroic Image	Organizing Content into Story Form
What "heroic" qualities or values are central to the topic? What makes the characters in this story full of wonder? In order to help students connect emotionally to the material, teachers need to first identify their own emotional attachment to it. What heroic human quality or emotion—courage, compassion, tenacity, fear, hope, loathing, delight, or whatever—can we identify in the topic? These "romantic" qualities help us—and our students—see the world in human terms and give human meaning to events, facts, and ideas in all disciplines. "Romance" invites us to view the world in human terms: not to confuse but to infuse the world with human meaning. Again, this first task is the most difficult part of planning the lesson or unit. We are asked to feel about the topic as well as to think about it; indeed, we are asked to "perfink" about it.	*What image captures the heroic qualities of the topic?* Images can be visual, auditory, tactile, gustatory, or olfactory. The central image for the unit should represent the transcendent quality that guides the unit by moving the story forward.	*What "heroic narrative" will allow us to integrate the content we wish to cover?* This is the trickiest part, and the part requiring the most imagination. "Think of the content of the curriculum more as great stories to tell than as objectives to attain. We might, then, think of 'story' much in the sense a newspaper editor asks a reporter 'What's the story on this?'" (Egan, *Arts as Basics*) Reflect on the whole unit or lesson and think of it in terms of some overall narrative structure. You want to select and highlight content that will make clear to students that one is not simply relating a sequence of facts or events, but that one has a story to tell them and that the set of facts and events have a unity of some kind. If you have listed a dozen possible heroic qualities, chose one that is central. Decide which elements in the content fit best into the narrative and fit with the central heroic quality or value and disregard the rest. It is often hard to let go, but it is crucial to remove unnecessary items that are not within the context of the story.

Developing Cognitive Tools

Exploring Human Strengths & Emotions	Extremes of Reality	Collecting & Organizing
How can students understand the human hopes, fears, passions, or struggles that have shaped our knowledge of this topic?	*What extremes of reality are related to the topic—biggest, hottest, oldest, richest?*	*What parts of the topic can students best explore in exhaustive detail? How can students present their knowledge in some systematic form?*
Think of how a good movie or novel makes aspects of the world engaging. Obstacles to the hero are humanized in one form or another, almost given motives; they are seen in human terms. To do this, we don't need to falsify anything, but rather we highlight a particular way of seeing it—because this is precisely the way students' imaginations are engaged by knowledge.	Children of this age are very engaged by the types of information that can be found in the *Guinness Book of World Records*. By finding the greatest and the least of something, they are establishing the limits of reality and thus establishing a scale to measure with. There are extreme examples within any topic. Perhaps when studying spiders it is best to first establish the largest spider, the most minute, the most poisonous, and so on before examining those that are less impressive.	While it is easy to give students a project to do that is part of a topic, it is a little harder to think about what aspect of the topic they might be able to exhaust, i.e., be able to find out nearly everything that is known about it. But there are such parts in every topic, and the security and sense of mastery that comes from knowing nearly as much as anyone about something is a great stimulus to inquiry. Think of something that is intriguing, that can be seen from a variety of different perspectives, or that is alluded to but not examined in detail in the content or in your teaching of it. Ensure that the topics which students explore in exhaustive detail relate back to the heroic quality. Otherwise, the humanized meaning will potentially be lost.

Looking Forward and Concluding

Toward Further Understanding	A Celebratory Ending	Assessment
How can the unit develop embryonic forms of Philosophic and Ironic understanding? What cognitive tools characteristic of the disciplines or embodied self-awareness can be introduced here?	*What is the best way of resolving the dramatic tension inherent in the unit? What communal project or activity will enable the students to experience and share this resolution?*	*How can one know whether the topic has been understood, its importance grasped, and the content learned?*
Consider questions one might ask about the topic from a Philosophic or Ironic point-of-view. These might be presented to students as "brain candy" throughout the unit or toward its end, or they might become more substantial areas of inquiry. Remember that students do not "graduate" from one layer of understanding and move suddenly into the next. Rather, they are probably more likely to experience a gradual shifting of a tendency toward or a proficiency in using particular cultural tools.	We will want to make sure that the unit ends on a positive note. One way to do this is to have students work communally on a project which resolves the dramatic tension of the unit. If we want the conclusion to lead toward Philosophic understanding, we might consider re-examining images we started with and reviewing the content through the lenses of other heroic qualities, which can give an opposite or conflicting image of the content.	Any of the traditional forms of evaluation can be used, but in addition, teachers might want to get some measure of how far students' imaginations have been engaged by the topic — how far they have successfully made a romantic engagement with the material.
(A unit at the Romantic level, however, will consistently emphasize and develop the cognitive tools of literacy even when some later tools are being introduced.)		Concluding activities can also be evaluative in nature. Remember, when evaluating, that the heroic qualities are what give us access to the content. These transcendent qualities are tools, and do not themselves have to be evaluated.

Appendix C

Philosophic Framework

Philosophic Framework   Topic:

Identifying "Great Ideas"	Acquiring Cognitive Tools		Tracing implications
	Close observation	Seeking and applying general schemes	
What great organizing or causal principles can be used to explain the topic? What gives the events or ideas around this topic an importance far beyond their own particulars?	*What features of the world pose the problem to be investigated and explained? What information about them best reveals the organizing power of general schemes?*	*How can general schemes be developed, applied, and tested within the unit? What features of these schemes make them particularly interesting, useful, or significant?*	*What does this way of thinking imply about the nature of the world and our relationship with it?*
The world is a vast and complex place. The search for underlying forms of order has been one of the perennial themes of human culture. Philosophic thinking infers the world from a grain of sand: by attending to particular instances, it seeks evidence of general schemes.	Every field of inquiry has its characteristic tools of investigation. Sometimes these are literally tools, as in many of the sciences (the microscope and telescope are two obvious examples). Sometimes they are tools in a more metaphorical sense: mathematical symbols, chemical techniques, psychological tests, methods of linguistic analysis. These tools capture the philosophical imagination when they uncover (or seem to) hidden structures or layers of meaning.	The wealth of information that becomes available as one focuses on a topic, perhaps using new investigative tools to do so, only becomes fully meaningful as it is used to develop, test, or apply general ideas. If these ideas seem to successfully explain one small sphere of experience, the philosophic mind looks for ways to apply them more broadly, or to define the range of their application.	Ultimately, philosophic understanding is bent on working out the essential characteristics of human existence: the possibilities and limitations of our ways of being, knowing, and acting in the world. Every advance in understanding seems to point to new terrain for exploration, new vistas of possibility.
The most difficult task here is to recapture the sense of possibility and discovery that was felt by earlier thinkers about a topic, before their work became simply part of the way we see the world (or was supplanted by a more successful narrative). The unit is then structured so that students themselves experience this narrative—so that the clarity eventually imparted by a successful general scheme is linked to the emotional satisfaction of discovery.			

Deepening Understanding		Conclusion: Theory Made Visible	Assessment
Introducing anomalies	Alternative schemes		
What problems confront the general schemes developed so far? How might they be dealt with? An important component of Philosophic understanding is an appreciation of the tentative and incomplete nature of all general schemes. One wants to begin with minor anomalies and gradually and sensitively challenge the students' general theory so that they make the theory increasingly sophisticated.	*What other general schemes have been or might be advanced to challenge the reigning narrative?* More challenging than isolated anomalies are completely different schemes for framing our thinking about a topic. If students can be challenged to respond to even one of these in some depth, it will greatly enhance their understanding and appreciation of the dominant scheme.	*How can the overall development of understanding in this unit be summarized and represented?* One wants to end a Philosophic unit in a way that makes the theoretical framework visible—enacted or represented in some way. This might involve a change in genre, for instance: using a literary theory to shape a dramatic performance, representing a scientific theory graphically or as a game, incorporating a social theory in a work of literature. If time allows, it might involve an original research project applying the theory to a case not explored within the unit itself.	*How can we know whether the content has been learned and understood, whether students have developed a theory or general idea, elaborated it, and attained some sense of its limitations?* In some ways this is easier than with Mythic or Romantic understanding, since Philosophic understanding involves making ideas explicit, justifying and defending them on the basis of evidence. One can involve the students in challenging one another (through debates, peer review, and other means), and one can examine their success in applying theories to new phenomena and in explaining away anomalies. The activities chosen for the conclusion of the unit should lend themselves to this kind of assessment.

Bibliography

Ausubel, D. P. (1968). *Educational psychology: A cognitive view*. New York: Rinehart & Winston.

Barrow, R. (1988). Some observations on the concept of imagination. In K. Egan & D. Nadaner (Eds.), *Imagination and education*. New York: Teachers College Press.

Bennett, J. G. (1967). *Systematics*. December.

Bettelheim, B. (1976). *The uses of enchantment*. New York: Knopf.

Brewster, D. (Ed.) (1855/1965). *Memoirs of Newton*, vol. 2, ch. 27. New York & London: Johnson Reprint Corporation.

Bruner, J. (1986). *Actual minds, possible worlds*. Cambridge, MA: Harvard University Press.

Bruner, J. (1988). Discussion. *Yale Journal of Criticism, 2*, 1.

Carey, S., & Gelman, R. (1990). *The epigenesis of mind*. Hillsdale, NJ: Erlbaum.

Coe, R. (1984). *When the grass was taller*. New Haven, CT: Yale University Press.

Coles, R. (1989). *The call of stories: Teaching and the moral imagination*. Boston: Houghton Mifflin.

Donaldson, M. (1978). *Children's minds*. London: Croom Helm.

Dunbar, R.I.M. (1991). Functional significance of social grooming in primates. *Folia Primatologica, 57*, 121–131.

Egan, K. (1997). *The educated mind: How cognitive tools shape our understanding*. Chicago: University of Chicago Press.

Egan, K. (2003). Start with what the student knows or with what the student can imagine? *Phi Delta Kappan, 84*(6), 443–445.

Egan, K., & Nadaner, D. (Eds.) (1988). *Imagination and education*. New York: Teachers College Press.

Eisner, E. W. (1985). *The educational imagination*. New York: Macmillan.

Frye, N. (1963). *The well-tempered critic*. Gloucester, MA: Peter Smith.

Gardner, H. (1991). *The unschooled mind*. New York: Basic Books.

Gardner, H. (1993). *Multiple intelligences: The theory in practice*. New York: Basic Books

Gardner, H., & Winner, E. (1979). The development of metaphoric competence: Implications for humanistic disciplines. In Sheldon Sacks (Ed.), *On metaphor*. Chicago: University of Chicago Press.

Gerofsky, S. (2004). *A man left Albuquerque heading east: Word problems as genre in mathematics education*. New York: Peter Lang.

Hayek, F. A. (1970). The primacy of the abstract. In Arthur Koestler & J. R. Smythies (Eds.), *Beyond reductionism*. New York: Macmillan.

Keil, F. (1989). *Concepts, kinds, and cognitive development*. Cambridge: MIT Press.

Kermode, F. (1966). *The sense of an ending*. Oxford, England: Oxford University Press.

Lévi-Strauss, C. (1962). *Totemism*. London: Merlin.

MacIntyre, A. (1981). *After virtue*. Notre Dame, IN: University of Notre Dame Press.

Maslow, A. (1970). *Motivation and personality*, 2nd ed. New York: HarperCollins.

McLuhan, M. (1964). *Understanding media: The extensions of man*. New York: McGraw-Hill.

Mills, S. (1990, May 11). Review of John Perlin's *A forest journey: The role of wood in the development of civilization*. In the *Times Literary Supplement*, p. 490.

Mithen, S. (1996). *The prehistory of the mind: The cognitive origins of arts, religion and science*. London: Thames & Hudson.

Olson, D. R. (1994). *The world on paper*. Cambridge, England: Cambridge University Press.

Pinker, S. (1994). *The language instinct*. New York: Morrow.

Shepard, R. N. (1975). Form, formation, and transformation of internal representations. In R. L. Solso (Ed.), *Contemporary issues in cognitive psychology*. Washington, DC: Winston.

Sutton-Smith, B. (1988). In search of the imagination. In K. Egan & D. Nadaner (Eds.), *Imagination and education*. New York: Teachers College Press.

Tyler, R. (1949). *Basic principles of curriculum and instruction*. Chicago: University of Chicago Press.

Vygotsky, L. S. (1978). *Mind in society: The development of higher psychological processes*. (Michael Cole, Vera John-Steiner, Sylvia Scribner, and Elaine Souberman, Eds.). Cambridge MA: Harvard University Press.

Winner, E. (1988). *The point of words: Children's understanding of metaphor and irony*. Cambridge, MA: Harvard University Press.

Whitehead, A. N. (1922/1967). *The aims of education*. New York: Free Press.

The Author

Kieran Egan was born in Ireland in 1942, but was brought up and educated in England. He read history (Honours) at the University of London, graduating with a B.A. in 1966. He worked for a year as a research fellow at the Institute for Comparative Studies in Kingston-upon-Thames and then moved to the United States to begin a Ph.D. in the philosophy of education at Stanford University. He worked concurrently as a consultant to IBM on adaptation of a programming method called Structural Communication to new computing systems. He completed his Ph.D. at Cornell University in 1972. His first job was at Simon Fraser University in British Columbia, where he has remained ever since. He is the author of about twenty books; coauthor, editor, or coeditor of a few more; and author of more than a hundred articles. In 1991 he received the Grawemeyer Award in Education. In 1993 he was elected to the Royal Society of Canada. In 2000 he was elected as a Foreign Associate member of the (U.S.) National Academy of Education. In 2001 he was appointed to a Canada Research Chair in Education and won a Killam Research Fellowship. Various books of his have been translated into about ten European and Asian languages. His recent books include *Teaching as Story Telling* (University of Chicago Press, 1989); *Imagination in Teaching and Learning* (University of Chicago Press. 1992); *The Educated Mind: How Cognitive Tools Shape Our Understanding* (University of Chicago Press, 1997); *Children's Minds, Talking Rabbits, and Clockwork Oranges* (Teachers College Press, 1999); *Building My Zen Garden* (Houghton Mifflin, 2000);

and *Getting It Wrong from the Beginning: Our Progressivist Inheritance from Herbert Spencer, John Dewey, and Jean Piaget* (Yale University Press, 2002). He is married with three children and, so far, two grandchildren.

Index

elaborated planning framework, 52, 55–56; electronic, 31–32; in Heat lesson, 72; in Homophones lesson, 66; in Properties of the Air lesson, 61
Play analysis. See "Hamlet" unit
Pliny, 136
Poetry, mystery in, 33, 34
Political campaign posters, 151–152, 154–155, 157–158
Politics, 158–159
Polynomial functions, 188, 189–190, 191
Pooh Bear, 77
Potter, Harry, 83, 108
Poverty, 117
Prairies, U.S., 116–117
Preferences, search for authority and truth in, 163
Pre-literate children, 77–78. See also Cognitive tools of language
Pre-service teacher education, 39, 86, 215
Prime numbers, mystery in, 34
Prometheus, 69, 70, 73, 74
Properties of the Air lesson: binary opposites in, 19, 59–60; conclusion of, 61–62; embryonic forms of later cognitive tools in, 61; emotional meaning in, 58; evaluation in, 62–63; mystery in, 62; planning framework for, 58–63; rhyme for, 21; story content for, 59–60; story structure for, 60–61
Ptolemy, 133
Public media, 172–173
Punctuation: mystery in, 34; teachers' emotional engagement in, 215–216
Pyramids, 98
Pythagoras, 101, 120–123
Pythagoras's Theorem unit: conclusion of, 122–123; evaluation in, 123; heroic qualities in, 120–122; narrative for, 120–123; planning framework for, 120–123

Q

Questioning, wonder and, 91–92

R

Realistic thinking, 77–78, 83–85. See also Cognitive tools of literacy
Reality: extremes and limits of, 78–79, 85–87; interest in heroes and, 79, 87–88; sense of, 78, 83–85, 221; sense

of abstract, 152–153; sense of wonder and, 79–80, 91–93
Records technique: for collections, 95; for Industrial Revolution unit, 118; for Parallel Lines Cut by a Transversal Form unit, 133; for Trees unit, 146
Redundancy, 68
Reflection, play and, 31
Relativity theory, 15, 183
Religion, 165, 181, 182
Renaissance, 189
Repetition, 192, 206
Revolt and idealism: characteristics and roles of, 101–102; classroom use of, 102–103; as cognitive tools of literacy, 81, 101–103; defined, 81, 221; in Trees unit, 147
Revolutions unit, 180–186; alternative general theories in, 184–185; conclusion of, 185–186; developing sense of agency in, 178, 185; evaluation in, 186; identification of general ideas/ theories in, 181; initial access to, 175–176, 181; introducing anomalies in, 177, 183–184; meta-narratives in, 167, 176, 181–185; organization and structure of, 175–176, 181–183; search for authority and truth in, 164. See also French Revolution; Industrial Revolution unit
Rhyme, rhythm, and pattern: characteristics and roles of, 19–22; classroom use of, 20–22; defined, 3, 221; for homophones, 20–21; in Mythic Framework, 225; for Properties of the Air lesson, 21
"Rhythm of Education, The" (Whitehead), 92–93
Ripley's Believe It Or Not, 86
Role-playing: to change context, 104–105; in children's play, 31; in elaborated planning framework, 52; in "Hamlet" unit, 199–200; in Mythic Framework, 225
Roman Empire, 143
Romance, 79, 92–93, 127, 228–230; in Eel Life Cycle unit, 138; in Trees unit, 146. See also Wonder, sense of
Romantic Framework, 227–230; embryonic tools of, 226
Rote learning, 200
Routine, classroom, 81
Rosencrantz, 198

Teaching with Fire
Poetry That Sustains the Courage to Teach

SAM M. INTRATOR AND MEGAN SCRIBNER,
EDITORS

INTRODUCTION BY PARKER J. PALMER
AND TOM VANDER ARK

Cloth / 246 pages
ISBN: 0-7879-6970-2

"When reasoned argument fails, poetry helps us make sense of life. A few well-chosen images, the spinning together of words creates a way of seeing where we came from and lights up possibilities for where we might be going. . . . Dip in, read, and ponder; share with others. It's inspiration in the very best sense."

—Deborah Meier, co-principal of The Mission Hill School, Boston
and founder of a network of schools in East Harlem, New York

Those of us who care about the young and their education must find ways to remember what teaching and learning are really about. We must find ways to keep our hearts alive as we serve our students. Poetry has the power to keep us vital and focused on what really matters in life and in schooling.

Teaching with Fire is a wonderful collection of eighty-eight poems from well-loved poets such as Walt Whitman, Langston Hughes, Billy Collins, Emily Dickinson, and Pablo Neruda. Each of these evocative poems is accompanied by a brief story from a teacher explaining the significance of the poem in his or her life's work. This beautiful book also includes an essay that describes how poetry can be used to grow both personally and professionally.

Teaching with Fire was written in partnership with the Center for Teacher Formation and the Bill & Melinda Gates Foundation. Royalties from this book are used to fund scholarship opportunities for teachers to grow and learn.

Sam M. Intrator is assistant professor of education and child study at Smith College. He is a former high school teacher and administrator and the son of two public school teachers. He is the editor of *Stories of the Courage to Teach* and author of *Tuned In and Fired Up: How Teaching Can Inspire Real Learning in the Classroom.*

Megan Scribner is a freelance writer, editor, and program evaluator who has conducted research on what sustains and empowers the lives of teachers. She is the mother of two children and PTA president of their elementary school in Takoma Park, Maryland.